Seeing and Being Like Him

Ron and Rebekah Coriell

Published Under Arrangement with
Fleming H. Revell Co.

A publication of
ASSOCIATION OF CHRISTIAN SCHOOLS INTERNATIONAL

P.O. BOX 4097, WHITTIER, CA 90607

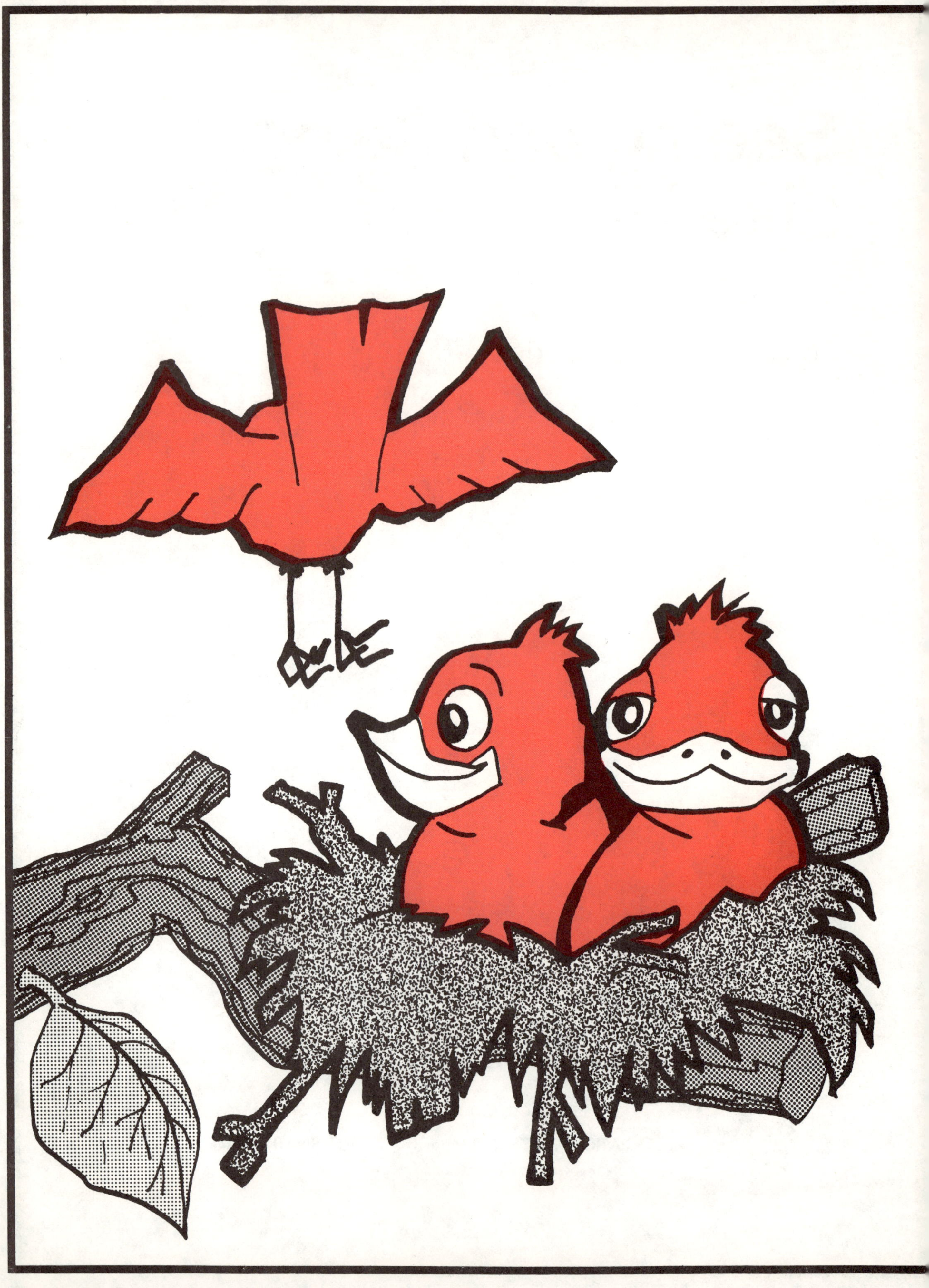

Obey
stay

**Doing What You Are Told
With a Happy, Submissive Spirit**

Obey them that have the
rule over you . . . .
          Hebrews 13:17

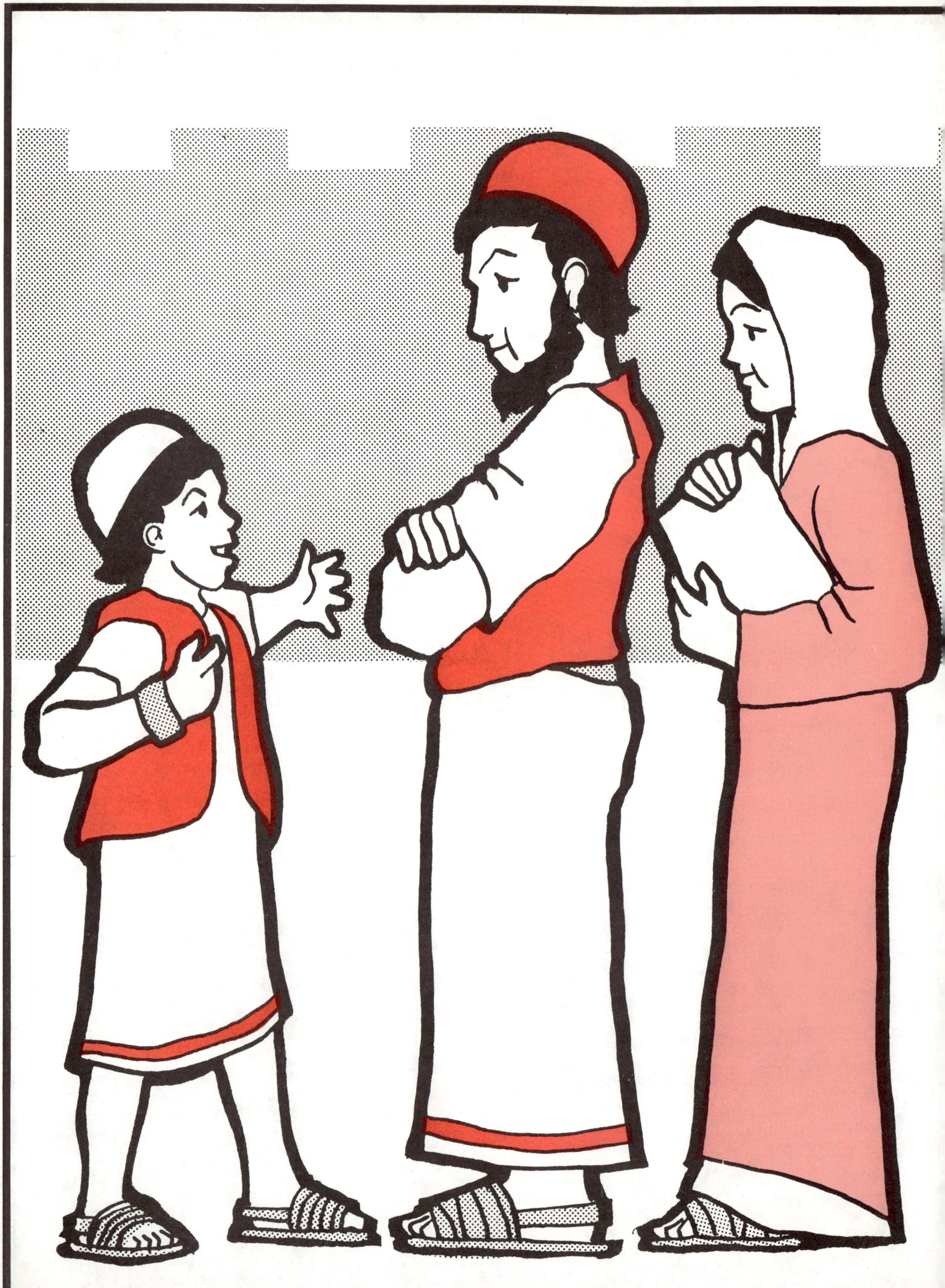

Obedience in the Bible

Once a year, the family of Jesus traveled to the city of Jerusalem to celebrate a special Jewish holiday called Passover. Jesus, a boy of twelve, went with them. When the feast ended seven days later, Mary and Joseph prepared to return home. They were traveling with many others, in a caravan, to be protected from robbers. His parents thought that Jesus was with them, but He was still in Jerusalem. It was a whole day before they discovered that He was gone.

Quickly they returned to Jerusalem. His parents began to look everywhere. At last someone directed them to the Jewish temple. There they found Jesus, sitting and talking to the teachers, who were amazed at His wisdom and knowledge of the Old Testament. His parents asked Him why He had not come with them. He answered that He must be about His heavenly Father's business. They did not understand this, but Jesus happily obeyed His earthly parents and returned with them to His home in Nazareth.

The Bible says Jesus was subject unto them. That means He did what He was told with a happy and obedient spirit. The Bible also says, "Jesus increased in wisdom . . ." (Luke 2:52). It is wise to obey.

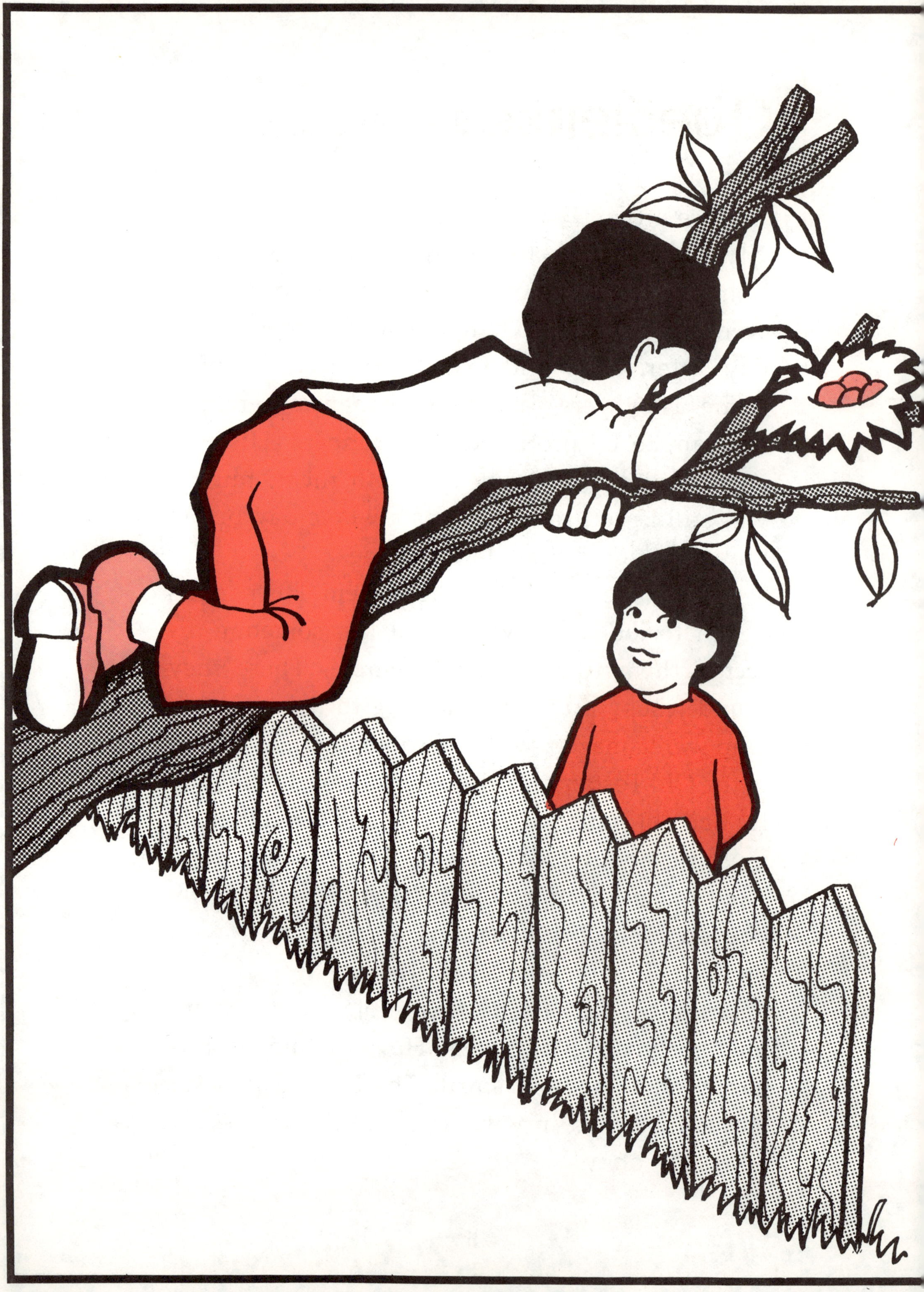

Obedience at Home

"Hey, Mike," shouted Billy. "Look what I found!"

Mike glanced up from playing in his yard, to see his friend Billy climbing out on a limb of the old maple tree.

"It looks like a robin's nest. Do you want me to show you the eggs?" said Billy.

"Didn't your father tell you not to climb that tree?" Mike responded.

"Well, yes," answered Billy. "I'll be careful. I'll put the eggs back before he gets home. Besides, you took four robin's eggs to school last week."

"I know I did, but didn't you hear what happened?" Mike replied.

"No, what happened?" asked Billy, as he stopped climbing just before reaching the nest.

"I was so proud of my robin's eggs that I showed them to everyone," explained Mike. "One of the eggs dropped when I was showing them to my friends. Two more were broken when I fell while riding my bike."

Mike continued, "Later, when my father found out, he had me place the remaining egg back in the nest and watch it. The mother robin wouldn't go near it. Father told me that birds will never return to their eggs when they have been touched by people."

"So that's why my father told me to stay away from our robin's nest!" Billy thought aloud.

"I had better climb down," Billy concluded. "There are many reasons why it is wise to obey Father's rules."

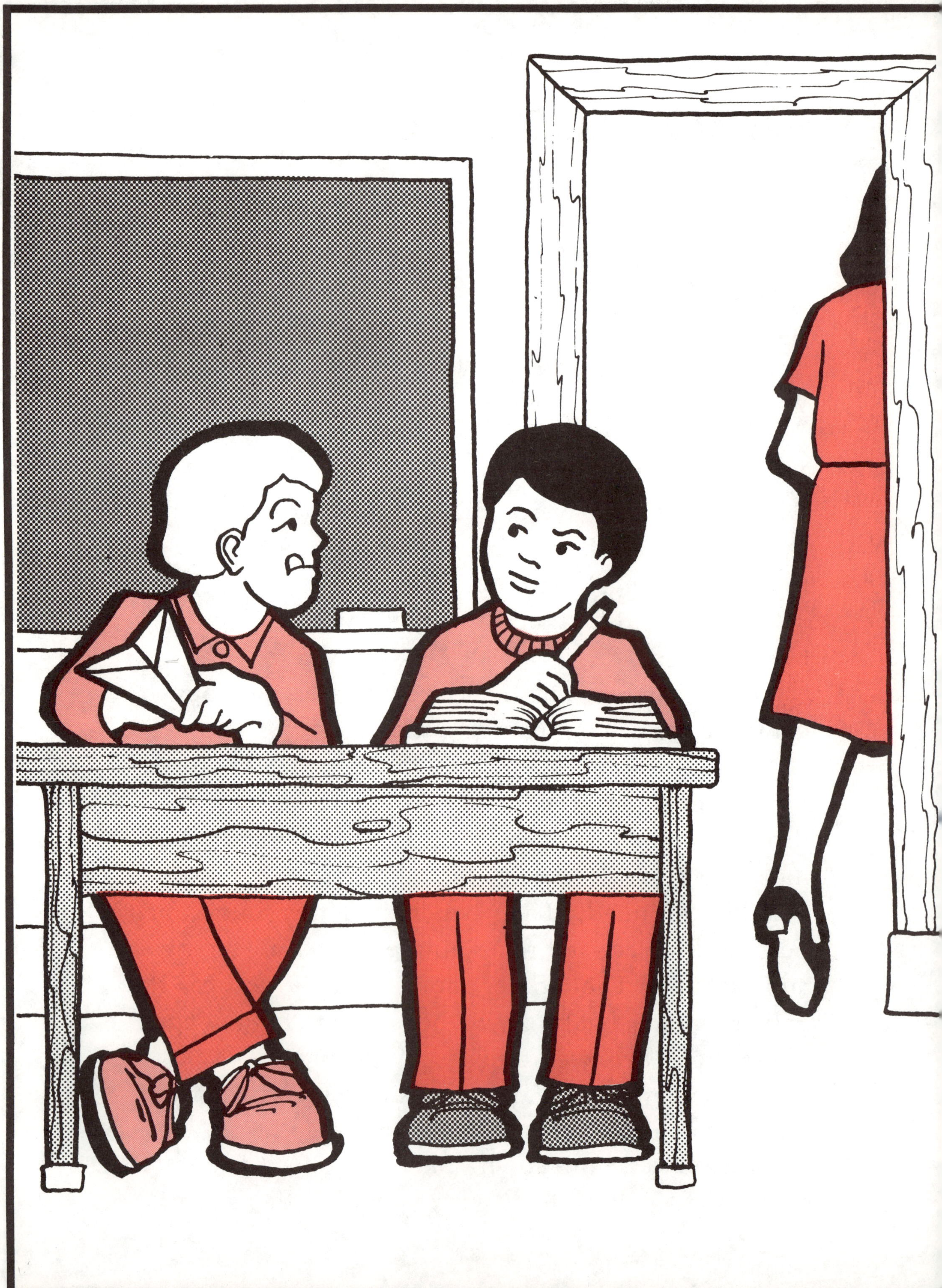

Obedience at School

A voice over the intercom asked Mrs. Harper, Billy's teacher, to go to the office. She told the class to remain quiet and finish their work.

Now is my chance to make the paper airplane that Billy showed me, thought Jeff. As Mrs. Harper left the room, Jeff started to fold a piece of paper into a plane.

Billy looked at his friend Jeff and was surprised. He thought, *Jeff just accepted Christ as his Saviour, at church Sunday. He should not be disobeying the teacher.*

Jeff had finished folding his paper airplane and was ready to fly it.

"Hey, Jeff," whispered Billy.

"What?" answered Jeff.

"Now that you are a Christian, you ought to know a special Bible verse. It has helped me to do right," explained Billy.

"All right, what is it?" asked Jeff.

Billy recited Proverbs 15:3: " 'The eyes of the Lord are in every place, beholding the evil and the good.' That means God is watching everything we do, wherever we are."

Jeff thought for a moment. Then he put the airplane in his desk and smiled at Billy.

"Thanks for helping me to do what we were told," said Jeff. "You are a real Christian friend."

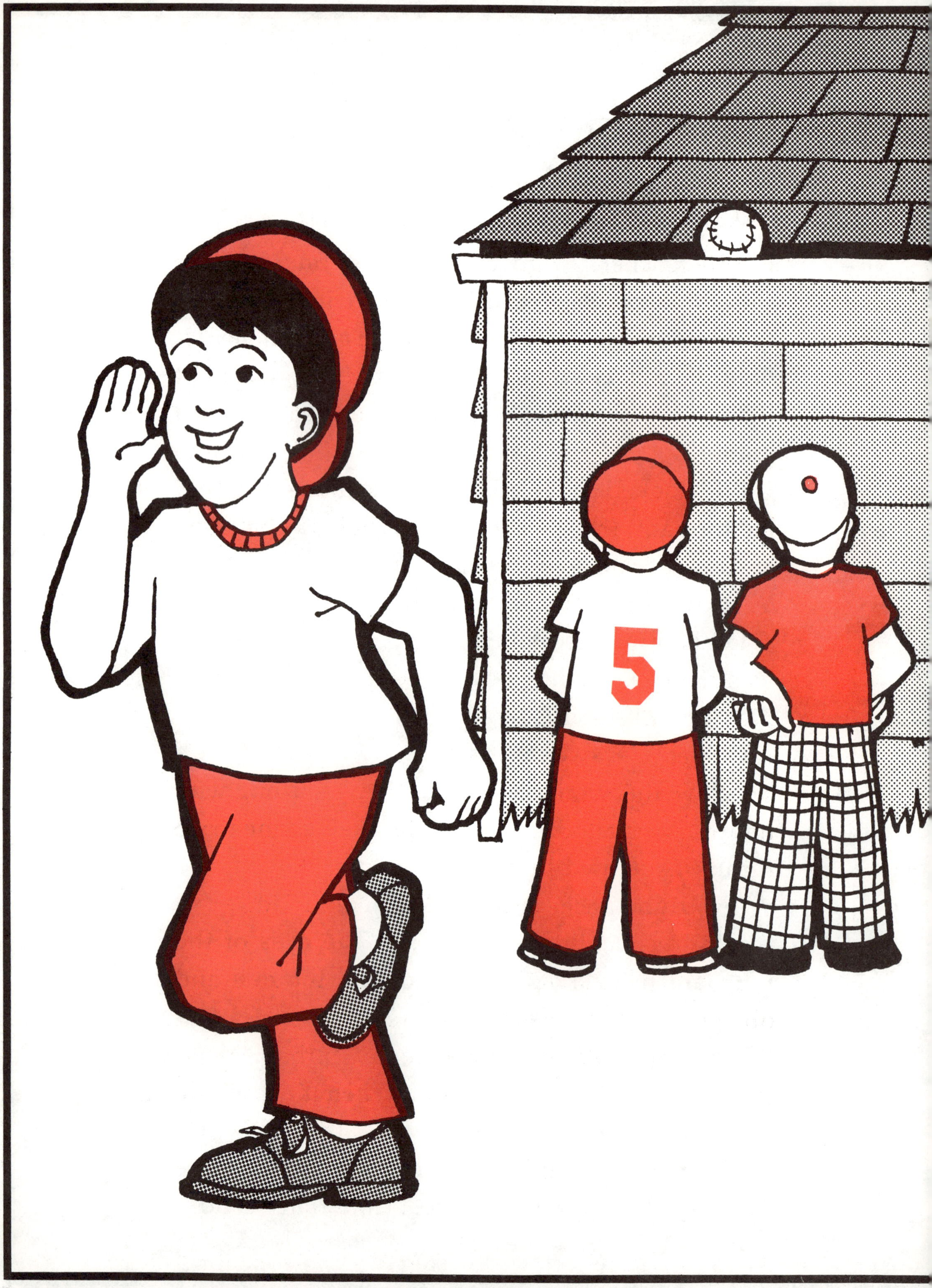
5

Obedience at Play

"Oh, no! It's stuck!" exclaimed Billy.

Billy had just hit a softball so high that it almost went over the roof of the shed. It hit the peak of the roof and rolled down into the gutter.

Billy loves to play softball. He can play it any time of the day and all day, if his mother lets him. One thing she will not let him do is climb up the shed roof. It is dangerous, she says, and his father has told him that he must call for help if a ball ever gets caught up there.

"Now, what are we going to do?" a friend complained.

"Well, we will have to do what my father told me to do," answered Billy. "Go for help."

Off he ran to find his father. The other boys shook their heads. They didn't understand why he couldn't just sneak up on the roof. Who would find out?

Billy came back with his father and a ladder. In a jiffy, the ball was retrieved.

Billy's father was so glad that his son had obeyed his wise words. As a reward, he decided to join the boys in their game of softball. Now, even Billy's friends are glad he obeyed.

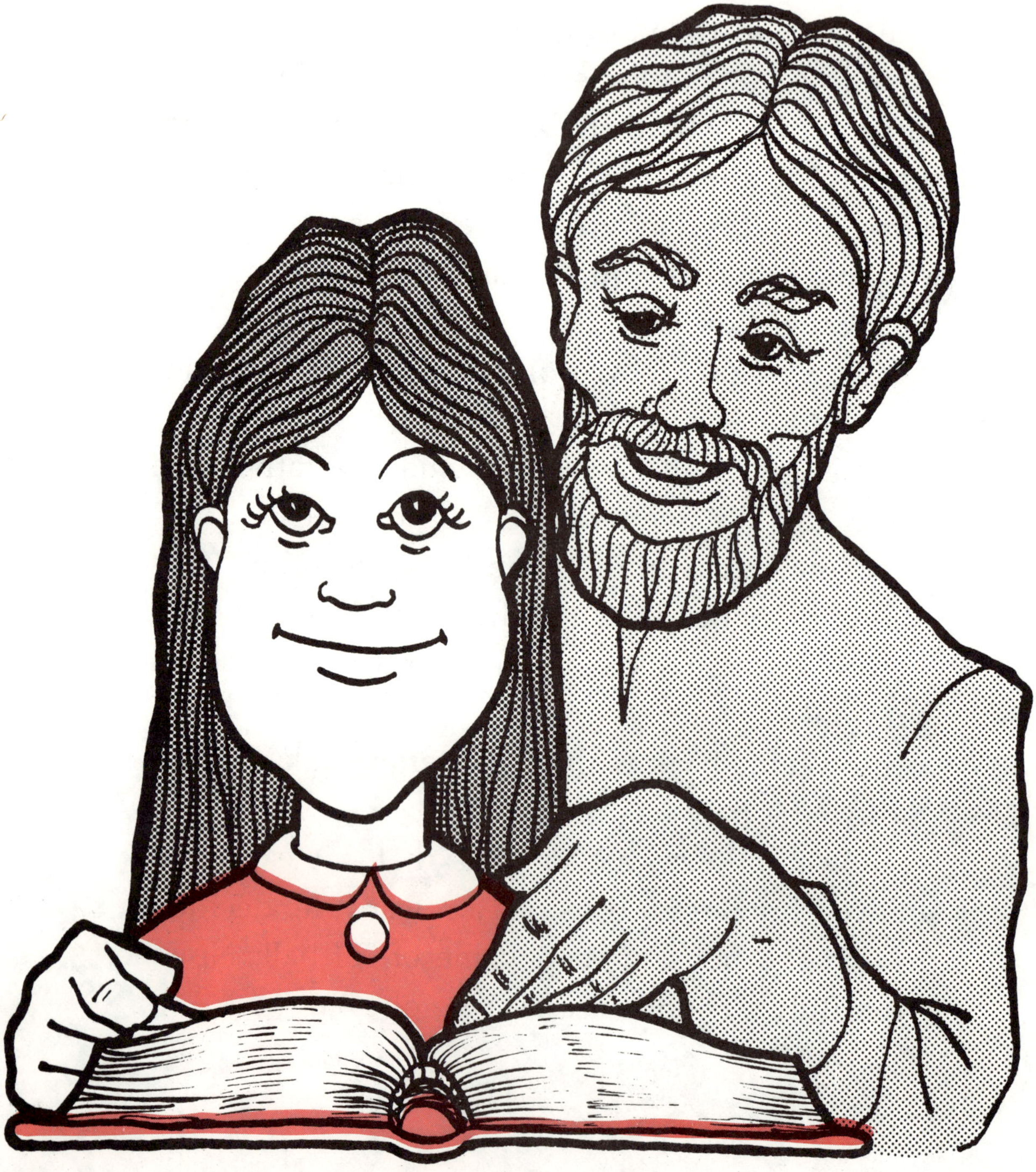

Wise
eyes

Thinking God's Way

Wisdom is the principal thing; therefore get wisdom. . . .
                    Proverbs 4:7

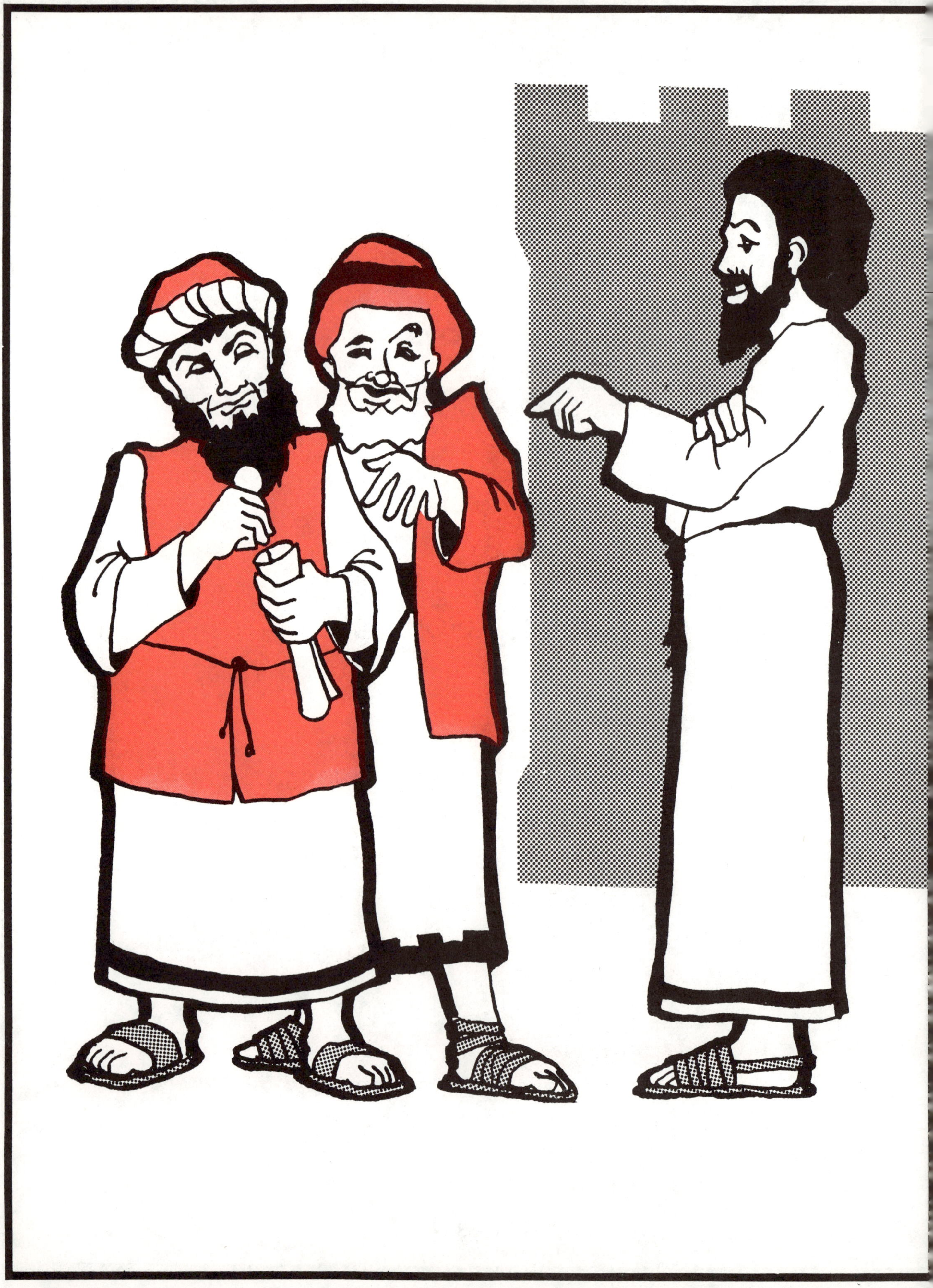

Wisdom in the Bible

The Jews lived in a land ruled by the Romans, who did not believe in God. The Jews hated their Roman rulers; some Jews also hated Jesus. The religious leaders did not believe Jesus was God's Son. They sent spies to try to trick Him.

These men came to Jesus with a special question. They asked Him if it were right for the Jews to pay taxes to the Romans. They hoped that He would answer *yes* or *no*. If He said *yes*, the Jews would be angry with Jesus. If He said *no*, the Romans would be angry with Him.

Jesus was a wise man. He always thought the thoughts of God, His Father. His answer was not *yes* or *no*.

Jesus said, "Show Me the tribute money."

So they brought Him a penny.

"Whose image is this?" asked Jesus.

They answered, "Caesar's, the Roman ruler."

Then Jesus said that they should give Caesar the things that belong to Caesar and give to God the things that belong to God.

Jesus had answered very wisely; no one could be angry with Him. When the spies returned to the Jewish religious leaders, they had nothing evil to report.

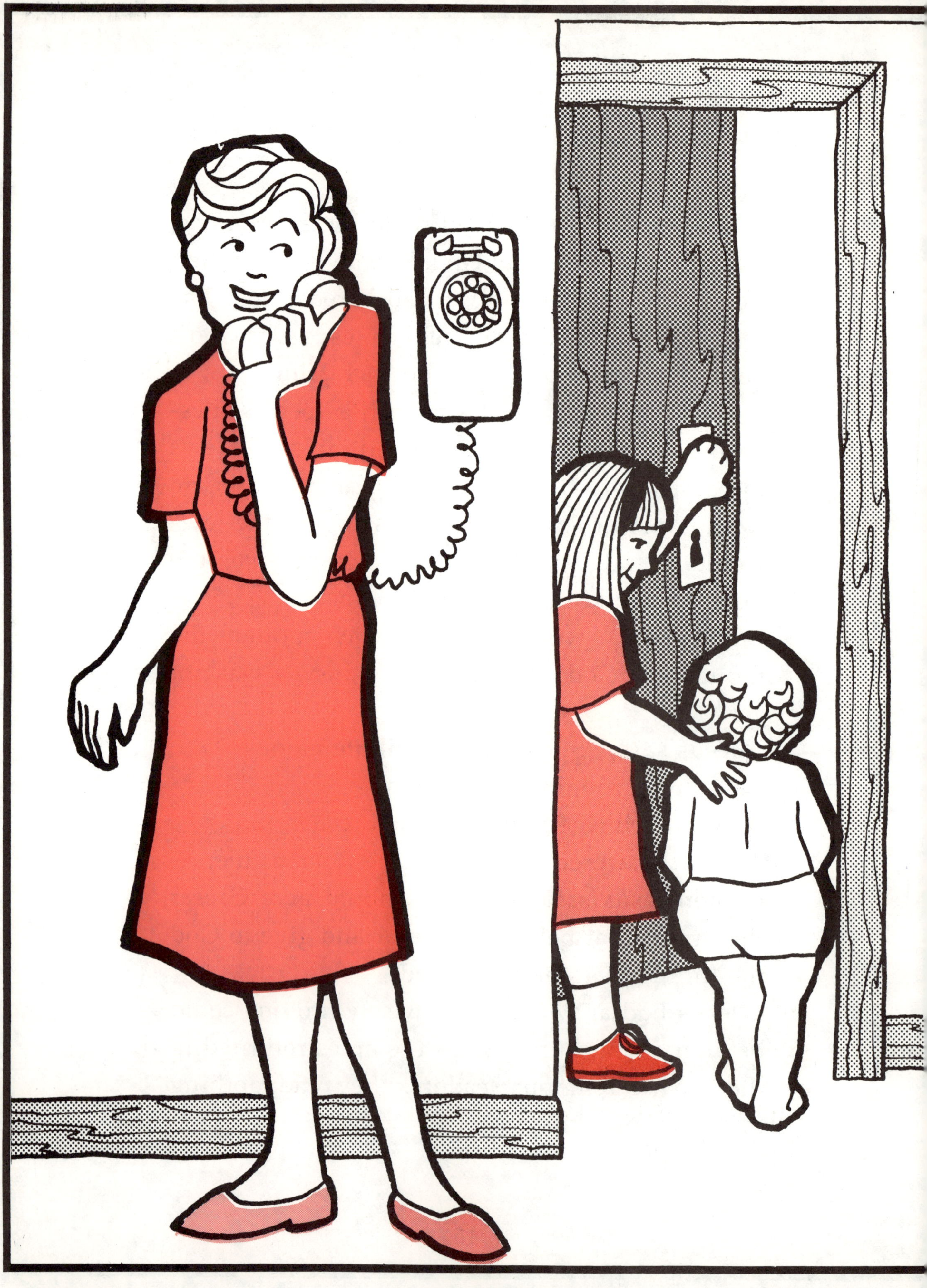

Wisdom at Home

Everyone in Wendy's family was sad. Father was going on a business trip. He would be gone a whole week.

Father reminded Wendy that she must be her mother's helper. Kissing everyone good-bye, he promised to telephone the following night. Everyone was sad to see him go, but it made them happy to know that he would call them soon.

The next day, everyone waited for the phone to ring. At last, it did. Mother answered. It was Father! Wendy's younger brother, Peter, became so excited that he started to cry. Wendy knew Mother could not hear Father's words, with all of Peter's crying. She knew that God's Word says, "Be ye kind one to another . . ." (Ephesians 4:32). She was sure it would please God if she played with Peter and helped keep him quiet, so she did. Mother and Father talked a long time, and Wendy had to give up her turn to talk.

When the call was over, Mother called Wendy. She said, "Wendy, you are such a wise girl. You helped me to hear Father's voice."

Wendy said she knew what God had wanted her to do. And it made her so happy to know her mother was pleased.

After Peter was tucked into bed, Wendy and Mother shared a plate of cookies and some milk, and Mother told her what Father had said.

17

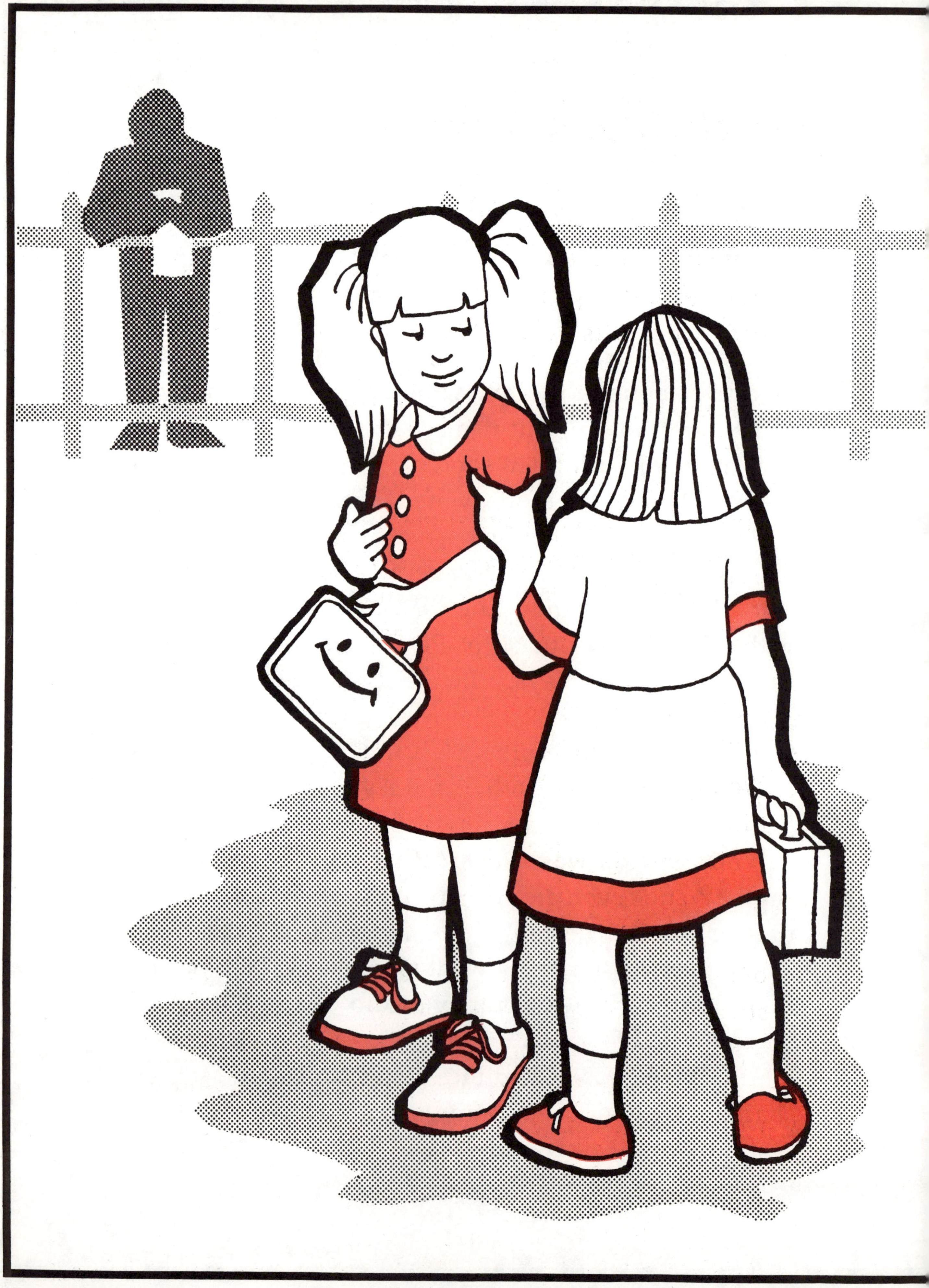

Wisdom at School

One Tuesday the weather was very hot. The principal decided it would be a special treat to have a school picnic. At lunchtime, all the children went outside to eat. It was such fun. Wendy and Samantha found a nice tree to sit under. The shade made it cool. When they finished, they decided to take a short walk in the school yard.

Just then, a strange man called to them. "Hey, girls, come here. I have something to give you."

Wendy had never seen him before. Samantha wondered if he might have candy in the bag.

"Let's go and see what he has," said Samantha.

She started to go toward him, but Wendy grabbed her arm.

"Mother told me never to talk to strangers," Wendy said. "We had better tell our teacher about him."

Mrs. Weber was so glad to hear how wisely the girls had acted.

"I know that God was very pleased that you obeyed the advice of Wendy's mother. Some strangers are not kind and might hurt you," said Mrs. Weber.

After hearing her words, Wendy and Samantha were very glad that they had been wise.

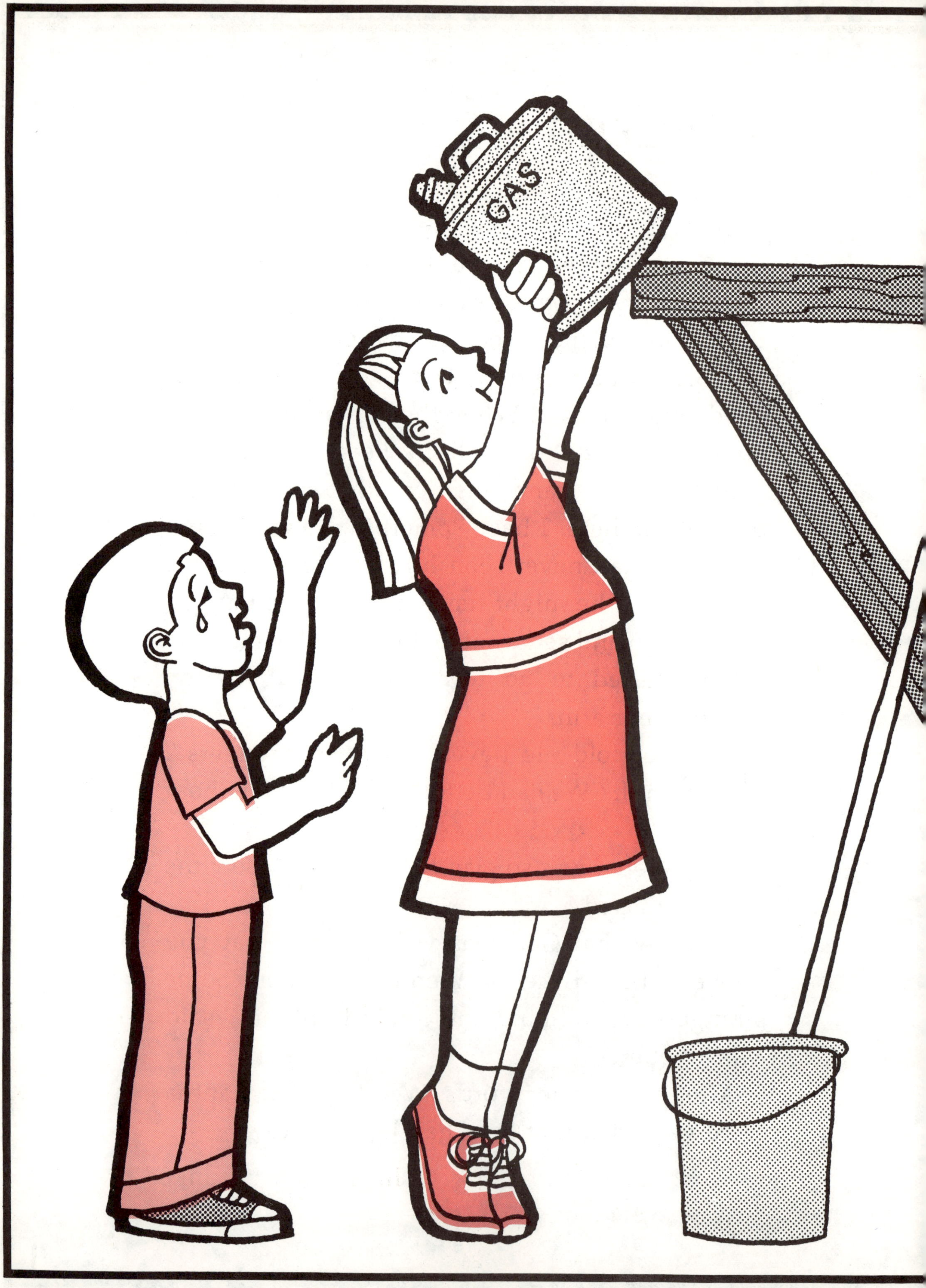
GAS

Wisdom at Play

Wendy's face was so sad. She looked out the window. All she could see was rain. It had rained all week. She wanted to play outside. She was tired of playing in her room. There were no more books to read, and all the table games had been played. She was even tired of listening to records.

Wendy went to her mother and sadly asked, "What can we do different today?"

Mother had a great idea. Father had just cleaned out the garage. She said they could play in there. Wendy shouted with glee! She and her brother, David, could even ride their bikes. Mother moved the car and told Wendy to watch David. Wendy said she would. Around and around they went on their bikes. They were having so much fun!

While they were playing, David picked up a bright-red can. Wendy knew this was Father's gas can, and it was very dangerous. Wendy knew God was watching her, to see what she would do. She also knew He wanted her to act wisely. So she decided to take the gas can away from her brother. She put it on a high shelf. Of course David cried, but she was happy she had done the right thing.

Father came home later that evening. He asked Wendy where his gas can was. She then told him what had happened. Her father smiled and gave both Wendy and David a big hug. In his heart, he thanked God for a wise daughter like Wendy.

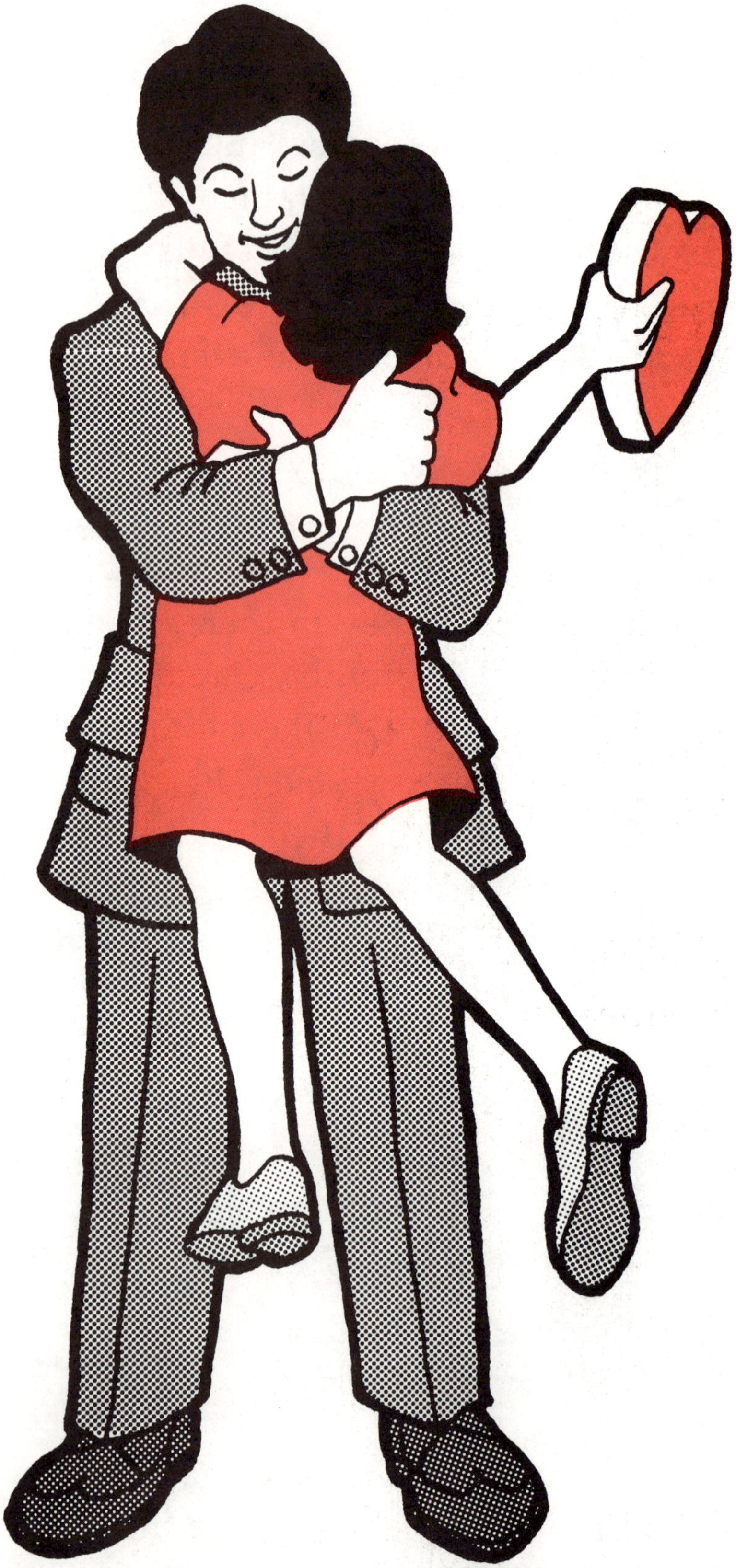

Tenderhearted
heart

Strong Enough to Feel the Joys and Hurts of Others

> Be ye kind one to another,
> tenderhearted . . . .
> Ephesians 4:32

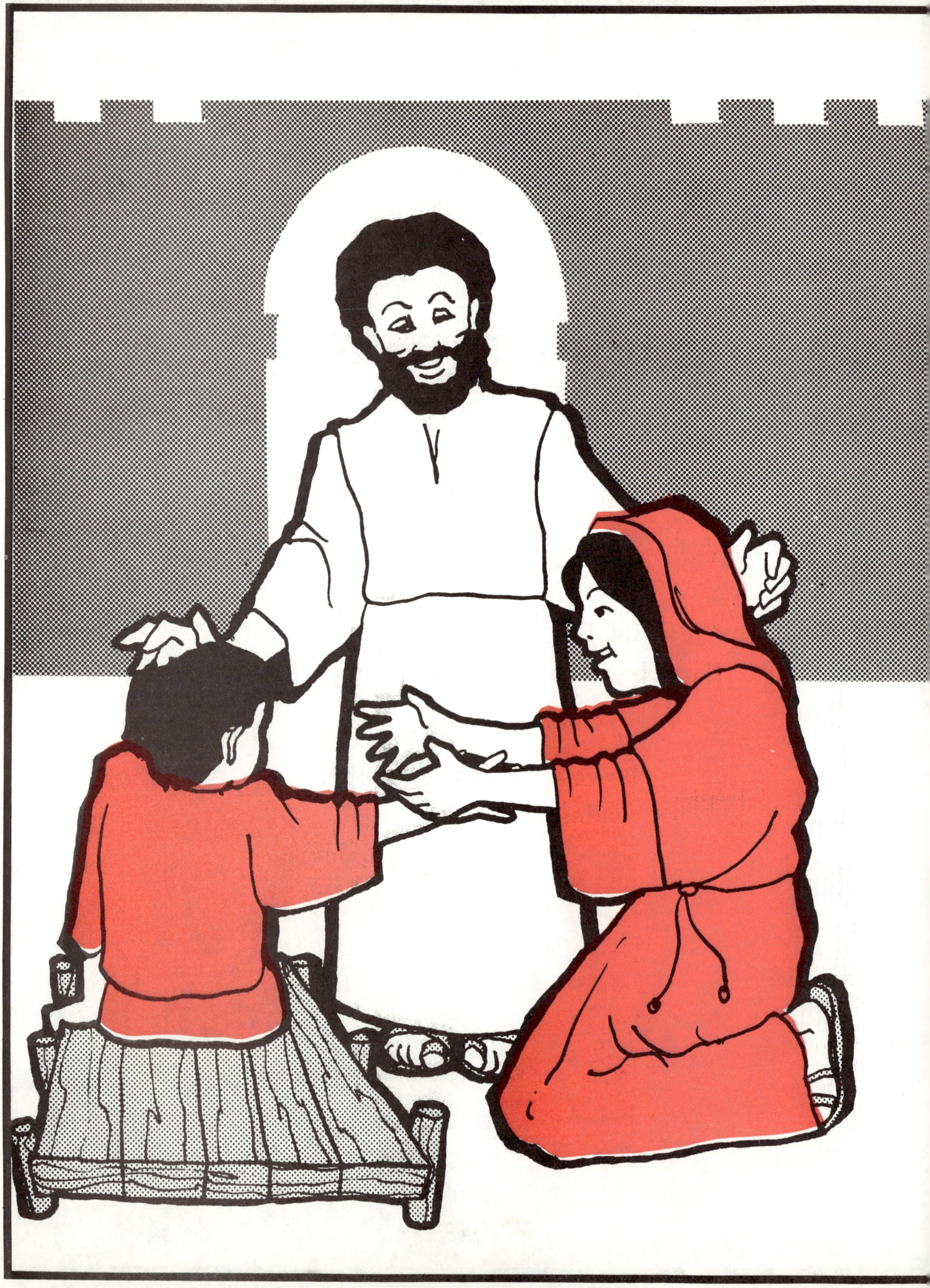

Tenderhearted in the Bible

As Jesus and His disciples were approaching the small village of Nain, they were halted by a funeral procession coming through the city gate.

"My son, my only son," mourned a widow as the body passed Jesus and His followers. Many mourners were following from the city.

When Jesus saw the mother, His heart overflowed with sympathy for her.

"Weep not," He said to her.

Then Jesus walked over and touched the casket. Looking in at the young man, He said, "Arise."

There was a great stir among the crowd when the young man sat up and began to talk! Jesus took him to his mother and reunited him with the rejoicing woman.

Jesus, tenderly, felt sorry for this widow. He was so moved by her great sorrow that He brought her only son back to life again.

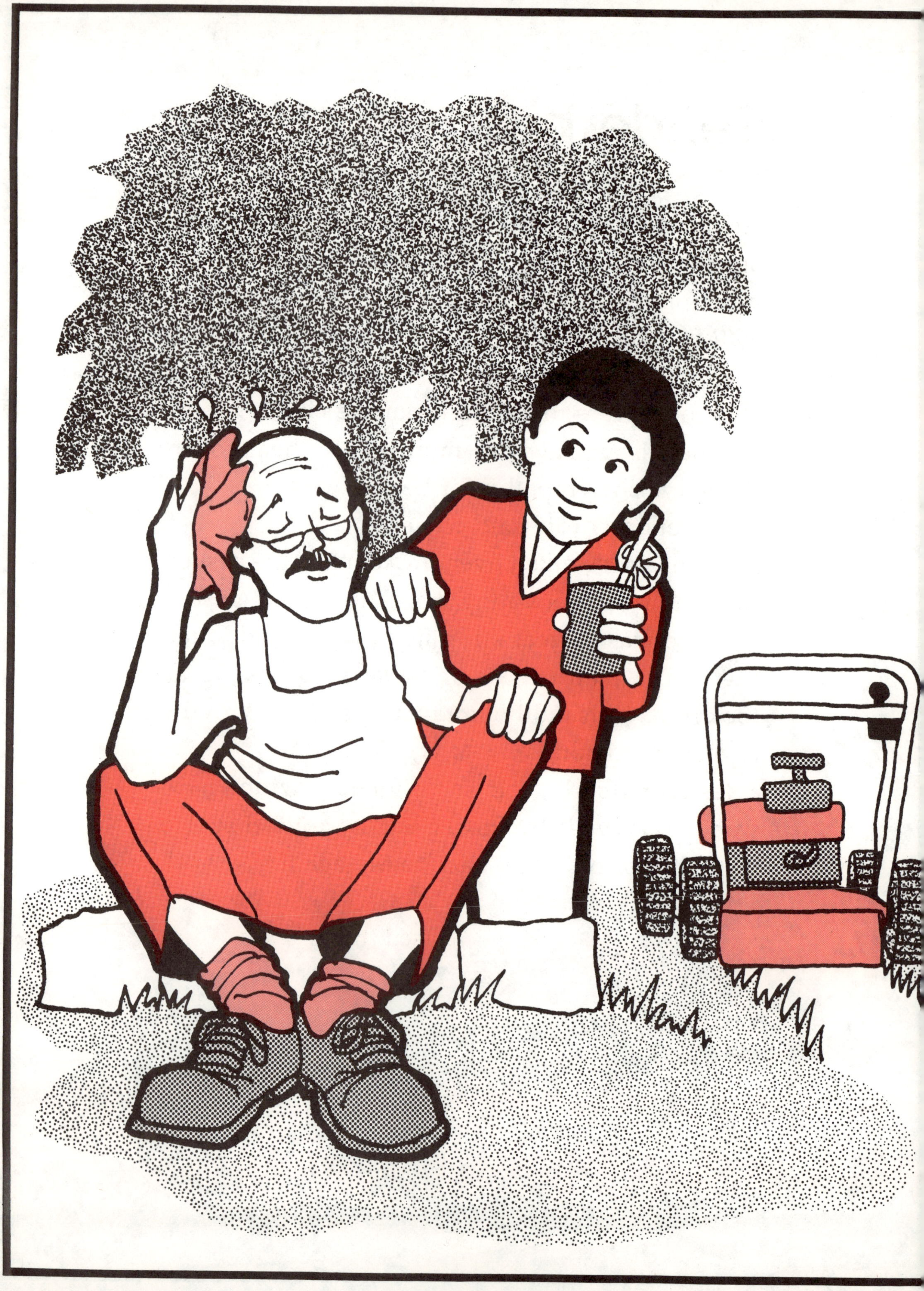

Tenderhearted at Home

Tommy's grandpa lived next door. Tommy loved to help Grandpa do all sorts of jobs. They raked leaves, washed the car, and even fished together.

One hot July day, Grandpa was mowing the lawn. The family reunion was to be at Grandpa's house. All the nieces, nephews, cousins, aunts, and uncles were coming. Grandpa wanted the yard to look neat.

As Tommy watched Grandpa mow the lawn, he noticed how hot and tired Grandpa was getting.

I wish there were something special that I could do to help Grandpa. There is only one lawn mower. And he is using it, thought Tommy. *I've got an idea!*

He ran into the house. A few minutes later, he came out with an ice-cold glass of lemonade. Grandpa was so tired that he had sat down on a rock and was wiping his brow with a handkerchief. Tommy offered him the lemonade.

Grandpa was very pleased that Tommy had been so tender. He was able to finish mowing the lawn because tenderhearted Tommy had cared.

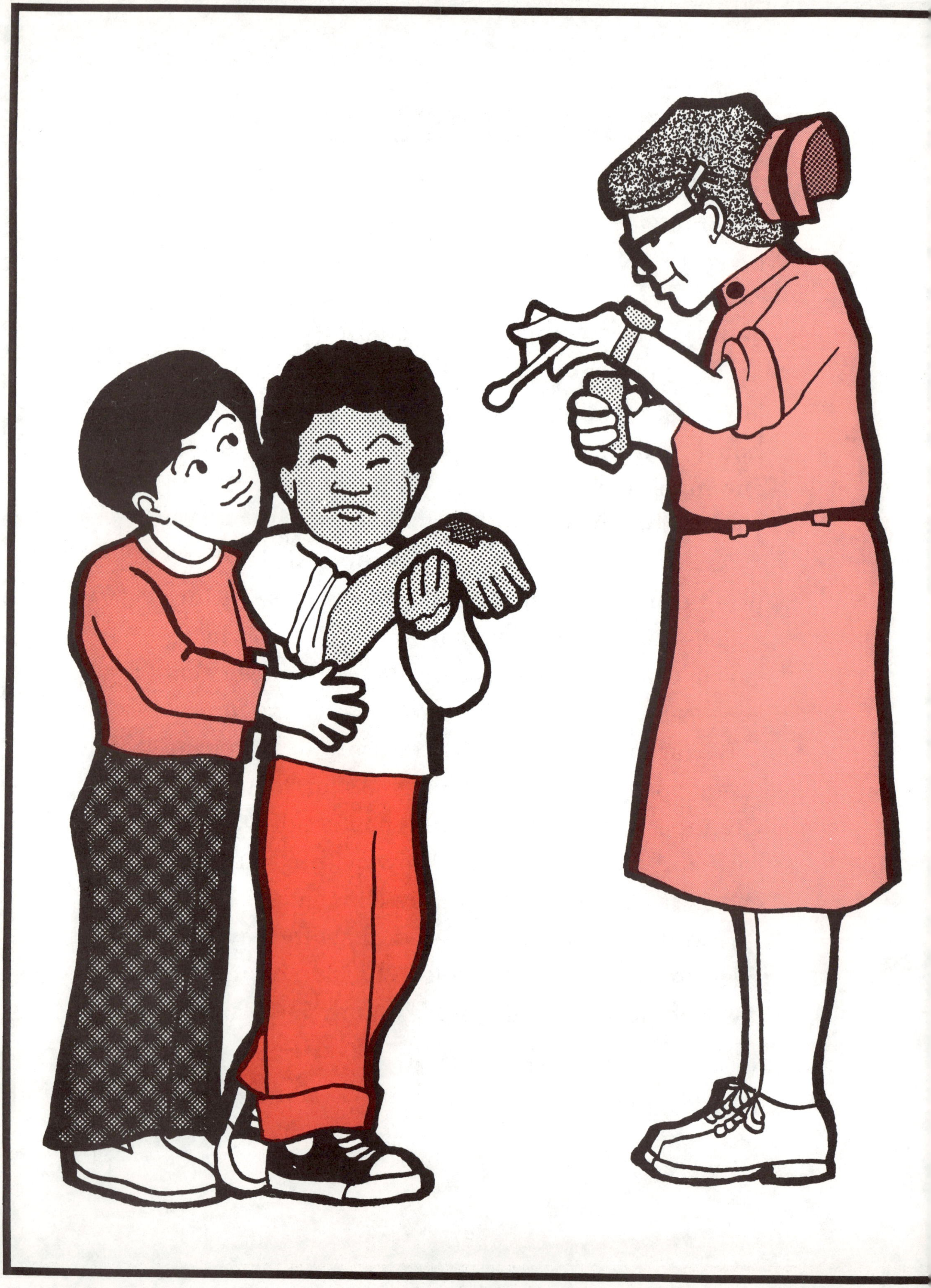

Tenderhearted at School

"Ouch, ouch, ouch!" cried Victor.

"Are you all right?" asked Tommy. "That must have really hurt."

Tommy's friend Victor had stumbled and fallen while playing tag on the school playground. His hand was scraped and dirty. Tommy saw how skinned Victor's hand looked, and he knew it needed quick attention. So he told Victor to go see Miss MaryAnn.

Everyone likes Miss MaryAnn, the school nurse. She is so kind and gentle. But no one likes to get a hurt hand.

"Oh, no! Not me!" Victor protested.

He was afraid that what the nurse might put on his hand would hurt worse than the scrape.

Tommy begged him to be brave and go anyway. It was best to get his hand taken care of properly, or later it would hurt even more. Tommy sensed that Victor needed to be encouraged.

"Look, I'll go with you. Maybe it won't seem so bad if we go together," said Tommy.

Victor agreed, and both went to the school clinic.

It took Miss MaryAnn only five minutes to clean Victor's hand and put a bandage on. And it didn't even hurt.

Victor was glad he had a friend like Tommy, who was tenderhearted and knew how he felt.

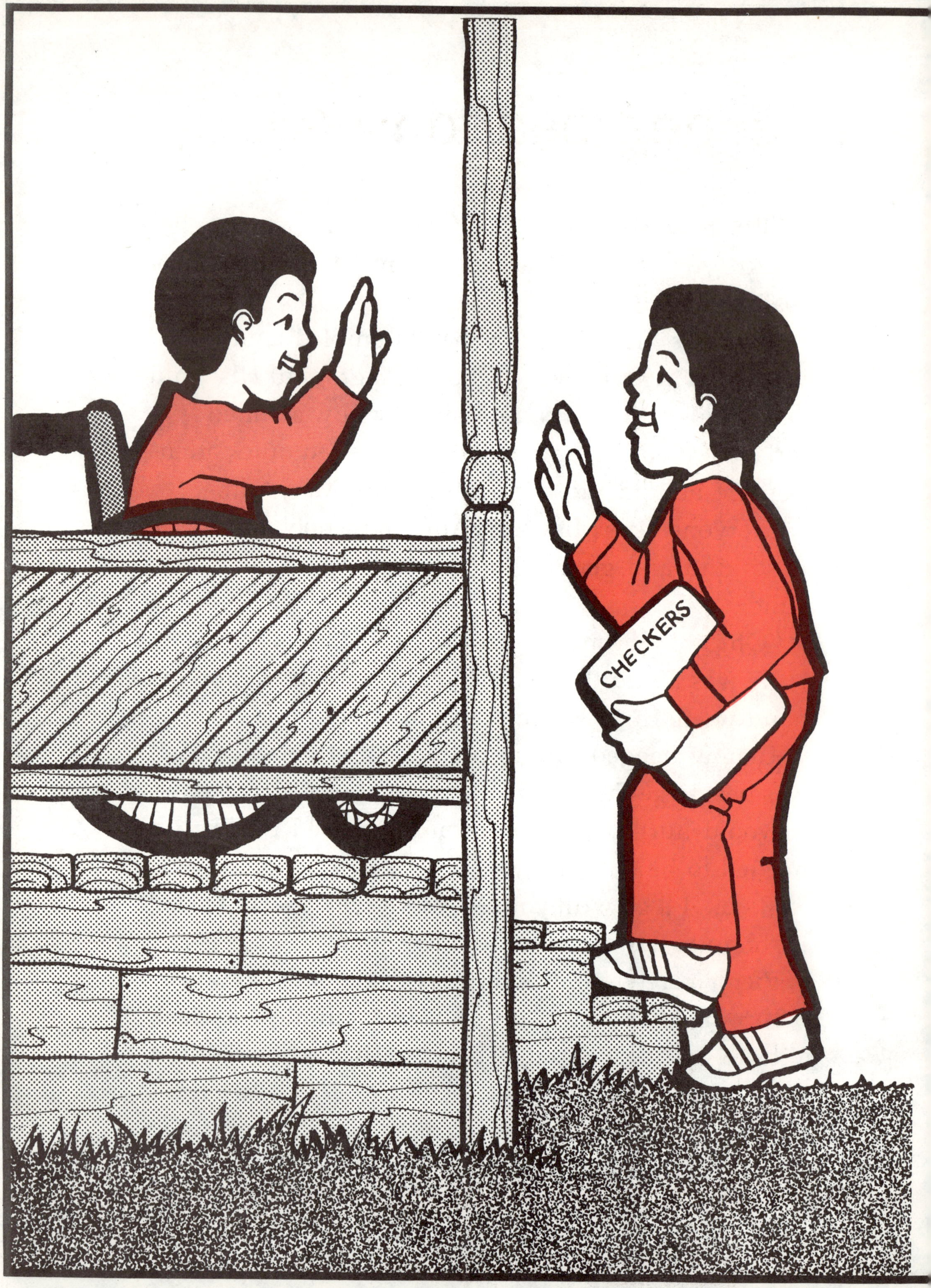
CHECKERS

Tenderhearted at Play

"It sure must be tough for Ike to sit all day in that wheelchair," said Tommy as his neighborhood soccer team passed Ike's house.

"Why can't he walk?" asked Joey.

"Before you moved here, Ike hurt himself while diving into a swimming pool," Tommy said.

The boys walked on toward the soccer field. Tommy looked back at Ike. He could see a frown on his face. Ike was sad that he had no one to play with.

Tommy remembered last summer, when his leg was in a cast. He could not run or play, so he had to learn to play quiet games, such as checkers.

Maybe Ike would like to play checkers, thought Tommy. *But what will my friends say? Will they call me a sissy? Will they laugh at me?*

Tommy looked at his friends. He looked at Ike. Then Tommy said, "Joey, you and the boys go play soccer. I am going to visit Ike."

Tommy went back to Ike's house. "Hi, Ike," said Tommy. "How would you like to play checkers?"

"Boy, would I!" said Ike, as Tommy came up the porch steps. "I was hoping that someone would play with me."

Tommy felt good inside, because he understood Ike's loneliness. Being tenderhearted, he was strong enough to make the right choice.

Character Development Challenges

This page is designed to give parents and teachers practical suggestions for teaching character traits to children.

Wisdom

1. Help the child memorize some Bible verses about wisdom (Psalms 111:10; Proverbs 4:7; James 1:5; Proverbs 24:3, 4; Proverbs 3:13).
2. The child should draw a picture of someone demonstrating wisdom.
3. The child should find out and tell how Solomon received his wisdom (1 Kings 3:3–14; 2 Chronicles 1:7–12).

Obedience

1. The parent or teacher should make a chart which children can mark using stars or stickers to show when they have obeyed.
2. With the child, discover a Bible character who disobeyed and tell what happened to him.
3. Teach the child to sing the hymn "Trust and Obey."

Tenderheartedness

1. Ask the child to cut out magazine pictures of people who need tenderheartedness.
2. Help the child act out the Bible story of the widow of Nain, found in Luke 7:11–17.
3. With the child, list five people to be tenderhearted toward and tell how to demonstrate this quality to them.

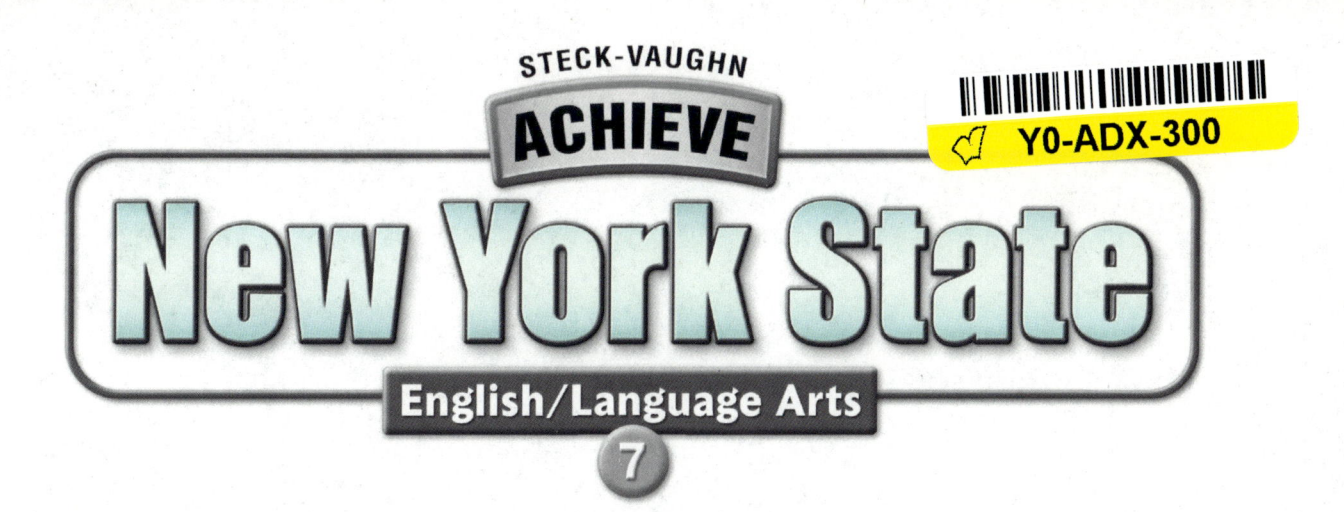

§ STECK-VAUGHN
ACHIEVE
New York State
English/Language Arts
7

Harcourt Achieve
Rigby • Saxon • Steck-Vaughn

www.HarcourtAchieve.com
1.800.531.5015

The New York State Testing Program in English Language Arts is published by CTB/McGraw-Hill. Such company has neither endorsed nor authorized this test-preparation book.

ISBN 978-1-4190-0941-9

© 2006 Harcourt Achieve Inc.

All rights reserved. No part of the material protected by this copyright may be reproduced or utilized in any form or by any means, in whole or in part, without permission in writing from the copyright owner. Requests for permission should be mailed to: Copyright Permissions, Harcourt Achieve, P.O. Box 27010, Austin, TX 78755.

Rigby and Steck-Vaughn are trademarks of Harcourt Achieve Inc. registered in the United States of America and/or other jurisdictions.

5 6 7 8 9 10 1413 11

4500285678

Achieve New York State
Contents

New York State English Language Arts Standards 2
To the Student: About Achieve New York State 3

NYS Testing Program Modeled Instruction
    Reading 4
    Listening 27
    Writing 31
NYS Testing Program Test-Taking Tips 32

Practice Test for New York State English Language Arts
    Book 1 33
        Session 1 34
    Book 2 53
        Session 2 55
NYS Testing Program Answer Sheet 61

New York State English Language Arts Standards

Standard 1: **Students will read for information and understanding.**
Students will write for information and understanding.
Students will listen for information and understanding.

- Understand stated information
- Draw conclusions and make inferences
- Use text to understand vocabulary
- Use knowledge of structure, content, and vocabulary to understand informational text
- Compare and contrast information
- Use punctuation and capitalization
- Use correct grammatical construction

Standard 2: **Students will read for literary response and expression.**
Students will write for literary response and expression.
Students will listen for literary response and expression.

- Determine use of a literary device
- Determine meaning of a literary device
- Use context to determine meaning
- Interpret theme
- Identify author's point of view
- Interpret characters
- Interpret plot
- Recognize how author's language use creates feelings
- Interpret setting

Standard 3: **Students will read for critical analysis and evaluation.**
Students will write for critical analysis and evaluation.
Students will listen for critical analysis and evaluation.

- Use critical analysis to recognize point of view
- Use critical analysis to evaluate information
- Use critical analysis to evaluate ideas
- Distinguish between fact and opinion
- Identify author's techniques
- Identify author's purpose

To the Student: About Achieve New York State

This book will help you prepare for the New York State English Language Arts Test. The first part of the book lets you practice the different kinds of questions you will see on the real test. It also gives you a tip for answering each question.

The second part of the book is a practice test that is similar to the New York State English Language Arts Test. Taking this test will help you know what the actual test is like.

The New York State English Language Arts Test includes questions about reading, listening, and writing. It will ask you to write about what you have listened to and read. It will also ask you to find and correct the mistakes in capitalization, punctuation, and grammar in a paragraph. Test questions will help measure how well you understand the skills outlined in the New York State Learning Standards.

Kinds of Questions

Multiple-choice Questions

After each multiple-choice question are four answer choices. For the Modeled Instruction part of this book, you will circle the letter next to the correct answer. For the Practice Test, use the separate answer sheet and fill in the circle that has the same letter as your answer. Remember to pick the choice that you think is the best answer.

Short-response Questions

These questions will not give you answer choices. You will need to write out your answers. These questions will be scored on reading and listening comprehension. They will not be scored on writing.

NYS Modeled Instruction: Reading

DIRECTIONS: In this section, you are going to read five passages. Then you will answer questions about what you have read. Circle the letter of the correct answer.

The following article describes early settlement in New York. Read the article "Colonial New York." Then do Numbers 1 through 7.

Colonial New York

What makes New York City one of America's richest and most successful cities? It is where George Washington was named the first president of the United States in 1789. The city was also the first capital of the United States until 1790. But the biggest reason for New York City's success comes from its earliest settlers.

In 1609, Dutch explorer Henry Hudson sailed his tiny ship, the *Half-Moon*, to the New World. He was looking for a shortcut to India. Instead, he found a river, which came to be called the Hudson River. He also located the mountains now known as the Catskills. Hudson and his crew continued to explore the wild, lonely land. They began trading food and furs with the Lenape (LÉN uh pee) tribes living on the shores.

When Hudson returned to Holland with news of the discovery, many merchants were excited. They realized that they could make a lot of money by trading and selling furs from the new territory. Merchants began to travel there, which was known by the Dutch people as New Netherlands. In 1626, Dutchman Peter Minuit bought Manhattan Island from the Algonquin people. There, he created a new trading post called New Amsterdam.

More settlers began arriving in New Netherlands. They settled near a Dutch fort, Fort Orange, and supplied food to soldiers. They formed a settlement called Beverwyck, and trading continued to be a successful enterprise throughout New Netherlands. Fort Orange, however, was destroyed in a flood in 1654.

Soon, the British got involved in settling this new territory. England and Holland had a long history of warfare, and in 1667, the Treaty of Breda was signed. The treaty allowed the British to take over all of New Netherlands from the Dutch. To set a more British pace, the tiny town of Beverwyck was renamed Albany. This name honored James, the English Duke of Albany.

New Amsterdam, the other early Dutch trading post, was still expanding. New Amsterdam's original population of 270 merchants and soldiers had grown quite a bit over the years. By the time the British took over, New Amsterdam was a full-grown colonial city. It was renamed New York in honor of the English royal, James, who was also the Duke of York. When James became King of England in 1685, New York became a royal colony.

Today, New York City remains one of the most thriving cities in the world. Albany, which is the capital of New York, can be a fun tourist destination. These two historic cities continue to impress visitors.

There are still remnants of Dutch history in New York State. Why, just outside of Albany lie the cities of Amsterdam and Rotterdam. The city of Schenectady was also an early Dutch settlement. The early settlers made quite a lasting impression on New York State. People continue to visit these cities to learn about Dutch heritage.

heritage = tradition

1 Read this sentence from the story:

They formed a settlement called Beverwyck, and trading continued to be a successful enterprise throughout New Netherlands.

In this sentence, the word *enterprise* means

A fort

B ship

C business

D settlement

🌀 **Tip:** When asked to figure out the meaning of a word, look at how the word is used in the sentence. Then look at the other words in the sentence. Decide which of these answer choices best fits the context.

2 Why did Henry Hudson sail to the New World?

F He wanted to explore new lands.

G He was looking for the Catskills.

H He wanted to trade food and furs.

J He was looking for a shortcut to India.

🌀 **Tip:** Information from an article can tell why people act in a certain way. Search the article for details about Hudson's trip to the New World to find out why he made the trip.

3 Which of these events happened first?

A The Treaty of Breda was signed.

B New York became a royal colony.

C Peter Minuit bought Manhattan Island.

D George Washington was named President.

🌀 **Tip:** Informational articles are often arranged in chronological order. Look through the article and find the dates on which these events occurred. Then decide which one happened first.

4 What settlement was formed near Fort Orange?

F Beverwyck

G New York

H New Amsterdam

J New Netherlands

🌀 **Tip:** When asked to find specific details in an article, identify key words in the question. Search the article for information about Fort Orange. Read the paragraph carefully to figure out the name of the settlement built there.

New York State English Language Arts Standards
1. **(1) Read for information and understanding.** Use text to understand vocabulary.
2. **(1) Read for information and understanding.** Understand stated information.
3. **(1) Read for information and understanding.** Use knowledge of structure, content, and vocabulary to understand informational text.
4. **(1) Read for information and understanding.** Understand stated information.

5 Which sentence from the article is an opinion?

- **A** "The city was also the first capital of the United States until 1790."
- **B** "Albany, which is the capital of New York, can be a fun tourist destination."
- **C** "It was renamed New York in honor of the English royal, James, who was also the Duke of York."
- **D** "The treaty allowed the British to take over all of New Netherlands from the Dutch."

Tip: An opinion is something that someone believes. It is neither correct nor incorrect. On the other hand, facts are statements that can be proved. Look over the answer choices to decide which one is the author's opinion.

6 Which of the following means the same as *remnants*?

- **F** new settlements
- **G** problems
- **H** visitors
- **J** bits and pieces

Tip: To find out what a word means, look at the words and sentences around it. Find the word *remnants* in the article, and decide what it means. Then think about which answer choice means the same thing.

7 Merchants were excited about Henry Hudson's discovery because

- **A** they were anxious to leave the Netherlands
- **B** they heard the new territory was very beautiful
- **C** they could make money trading and selling furs
- **D** they would be able to provide food to soldiers

Tip: Authors include details that help explain why events happen or why people react a certain way. Search the article to find out the merchants' reaction to Hudson's discovery. Look at the sentences near it to determine why they were excited.

New York State English Language Arts Standards
5. (3) **Read for critical analysis and evaluation.** Distinguish between fact and opinion.
6. (1) **Read for information and understanding.** Use text to understand vocabulary.
7. (1) **Read for information and understanding.** Understand stated information.

Read this story about the Civil Rights Movement. Then do Numbers 8 through 14.

A March to Remember

March 21

Dear Roxanne,

I was very happy to receive your letter last week. Your mama and I were the closest of cousins growing up. Of course, we're still close despite my living a thousand miles away from Selma. But it just isn't the same. And now here you are, writing to me with your request for information!

In 1964 I was about your age. At the time, most everything in Selma was black and white. I don't mean like an old movie. I mean there were drinking fountains and restaurants and swimming pools for white people, and there were different ones for black people. Even the voting situation was black and white: white people could easily exercise their right to vote, and black people couldn't. Lots of rules and regulations, and some outright threats, had been made to keep black people from voting.

I'm not sure what shook me awake that summer of 1964. Maybe I just started paying attention. I began to hear about the Student Nonviolent Coordinating Committee. That group had people from all parts of the country working in the South to get African Americans registered to vote.

Then the next January, Dr. King came to town and preached at our church. Everyone walked out of that service positively glowing with the energy to get some changes made. Dr. King's words touched even my mama and daddy, who had always seemed reluctant to rock any boat.

A few weeks later the voting rights activists planned a march along Highway 80 from our town to Montgomery. They were going to sing out their grievances on the capitol steps, and I planned to sing with them. But my mama and daddy refused to let their little girl jump into such a risky situation. I was heartbroken.

grievances = complaints

My folks were right about the risk. The marchers hadn't gone more than six blocks when Alabama and Selma policemen forcibly stopped them at the Edmund Pettus Bridge. I'll never forget the phone calls that night. Friends and relatives up North wanted to know if we were all right, if we'd been hurt in that awful confrontation they'd seen on the news.

You should have seen Selma after that! The streets were full of strangers who had come to support our voting rights. When I found out that another march had been planned, I announced to Mama and Daddy that nothing was going to stop me from being in it. It turned out that the second march, led by Dr. King, was peaceful—really just a symbolic action.

Finally, the civil rights leaders asked a federal court for protection for the marchers along their route to Montgomery. A judge declared that the marchers had the constitutional right to protest injustice by marching down the highway to the state capitol. About that same time, the President went on TV and told the whole country that we desperately needed laws to assure that black people could vote.

By now, a great deal of excitement was rippling through Selma. We had a federal judge and the President on our side.

As you can expect, I asked my parents for permission to join the third march to Montgomery. They knew that, with the court decision, this time would be different. Besides, half my aunts and uncles and cousins were planning to march.

On today's very date in 1965, over 3,000 of us set off from my church. The next five days and 54 miles were the most glorious time and distance I've ever passed through. We were so caught up in a sense of community, righteous cause, and jubilation that we hardly noticed our sore feet. We sang as we marched, and I came to believe that our singing went out into the universe and awoke people from a deep slumber. Thousands of people joined. By the time we were at the Capitol, we were 25,000 strong. Standing in that crowd, listening to Dr. King's powerful words, I could almost sense the future splitting away from the past.

You must have read in some history book what happened not long afterward. Congress passed the laws President Johnson had wanted, and in August he signed the Voting Rights Act. But, you know, facts like that are pallid compared to the bright-colored events leading up to them—events that I lived through.

I hope my story helps you with your history report. Please write again. And give your mama a tremendous hug for me.

Love,

Aunt Jackie

8 The author includes the second paragraph in the story to

F describe the state of the country during the 1960s

G create sympathy for Aunt Jackie

H present a point of view different from Aunt Jackie's

J describe life in Selma before the marches

Tip: An author sometimes presents background information that he or she believes is important to the plot. Reread the paragraph. Consider why Aunt Jackie would want her niece to know this information.

9 Read these sentences from the passage:

Congress passed the laws President Johnson had wanted, and in August he signed the Voting Rights Act. But, you know, facts like that are pallid compared to the bright-colored events leading up to them—events that I lived through.

As it is used above, what does *pallid* mean?

A more reliable

B less interesting

C exciting

D useless

Tip: When looking for the meaning of an unfamiliar word, pay close attention to nearby words and sentences. Reread the sentences carefully, and think about the comparison the author makes.

10 Which sentence from the story shows that the policemen's violence against the first marchers did not have the desired effect?

F "Then the next January, Dr. King came to town and preached at our church."

G "They were going to sing out their grievances on the capitol steps, and I planned to sing with them."

H "I began to hear about the Student Nonviolent Coordinating Committee."

J "The streets were full of strangers who had come to support our voting rights."

Tip: Use the information from the text and your own knowledge to answer the question. Think about what probably upset the police as a result of the confrontation. Then think about what happened next in Selma.

11 The tone of this story is

A jubilant

B bitter

C sentimental

D regretful

Tip: The tone of a story reflects how the author feels or thinks about a subject. When a story is written in the first person, an author usually discusses his or her point of view. Look for words and phrases that provide clues about Aunt Jackie's feelings. This will help you determine the tone of the story.

New York State English Language Arts Standards
8. (3) **Read for critical analysis and evaluation.** Identify author's purpose.
9. (2) **Read for literary response and expression.** Use context to determine meaning.
10. (3) **Read for critical analysis and evaluation.** Use critical analysis to evaluate information.
11. (2) **Read for literary response and expression.** Recognize how author's language use creates feelings.

12 In the sentence, "Our singing went into the universe and awoke people from a deep slumber," the phrase *deep slumber* means

    F a lack of awareness

    G a strong prejudice

    H a peaceful attitude

    J a solid night's sleep

> **Tip:** Sometimes authors use descriptive language to help readers get a clearer picture of ideas. Look closely at how the words are used in the sentence, and think beyond the dictionary definitions of the words.

13 From the story, the reader can conclude that

    A Aunt Jackie has moved away from Selma, and she misses living there

    B Selma is a good example of what the South was like in the 1960s

    C the events that happened in Selma affected Aunt Jackie's actions

    D Aunt Jackie wants Roxanne to appreciate the town where she grew up

> **Tip:** The theme of a story is the most important idea supported throughout the text. When you are asked to draw a conclusion about a theme of a story, think about the evidence from the story that can support each answer choice. Then decide which answer choice is best supported in the text.

14 Which sentence from the story is an opinion?

    F "On today's very date in 1965, over 3,000 of us set off from my church."

    G "The next five days and 54 miles were the most glorious time and distance I've ever passed through."

    H "Congress passed the laws President Johnson had wanted, and in August he signed the Voting Rights Act."

    J "In 1964 I was about your age."

> **Tip:** An author can blend facts and opinions when telling about a personal experience. Remember that a fact is information that can be proved to be true, and an opinion is how a person feels about something. Consider which sentence shows how Aunt Jackie feels about something.

New York State English Language Arts Standards
12. (3) **Read for critical analysis and evaluation.** Identify author's techniques.
13. (2) **Read for literary response and expression.** Interpret theme.
14. (3) **Read for critical analysis and evaluation.** Distinguish between fact and opinion.

Read the following article about large reptiles, alligators and crocodiles. Then do Numbers 15 through 25.

Reptile Brothers— Alligators and Crocodiles

People who live in southern Florida are never surprised to learn that they have a new neighbor at their local pond or lake. With a long body and broad "smile," this new resident is usually not welcome. Why? Because he's probably an American alligator, and most people would prefer that he go someplace else. You may know that alligators live all over the southern United States and that Florida has the most of them.

You might not know, however, that there are also crocodiles in Florida. Next time you're in the Sunshine State, remember these tips. They will help you to tell the two fearsome creatures apart.

The main difference between alligators and crocodiles is the shape of their snout. Alligators have a broad "U"-shaped snout. The snout of the crocodile is pointier, more like a "V." The alligator's snout is designed to be very strong. This is because alligators use their powerful jaws to crack the shells of animals like turtles. Turtles and other hard-shelled animals make up a large part of their diet. Crocodile jaws are also very strong, but scientists think their snouts might be a little narrower so that the crocodiles can eat a wider variety of prey. For example, crocodiles often eat more fish than alligators do. The crocodile's slimmer snout is better for catching fish.

There is another difference between crocodiles and alligators. It's the way their teeth look. An alligator's teeth on his lower jaw are hidden when his mouth is closed. A crocodile, on the other hand, looks more "toothy" with a closed mouth. If you look closely, you can see that the teeth on the upper and lower jaws of a crocodile interlock like puzzle pieces. There is also something special about the bottom jaw's fourth tooth. It arcs upward to the top jaw like a large fang.

Alligators and crocodiles usually live in different habitats. Crocodiles prefer brackish water, which contains some salt. Fresh water contains none. Both crocodiles and alligators have a gland in their mouths that helps them clean salt out of the water they live in. But crocodiles can live more easily in salty waters because the gland works better for them. Alligators prefer fresh water. This is probably why they are more likely to turn up in Florida's many man-made ponds and canals. Florida alligators have been known to stroll across golf courses, new housing developments, and even college campuses, moving from one body of fresh water to another. They have even been found in swimming pools!

habitats = environments

Finally, crocodiles and alligators have special organs on their skin that tell them when the pressure of the water around them has changed because prey is close by. These organs look like little black speckles or dots. A crocodile has these "sense organs" all over his body. An alligator only has them on his jaws.

Although alligators and crocodiles have a few differences, they also have many things in common. To begin with, they both belong to a larger group of reptiles called "crocodilians." So, in a way, they are like siblings.

Crocodilians have excellent hearing. Their ears are covered with small slits that close up when they dive. They can also see very well when their eyes are above water. Crocodilians' eyes sit on the top of their heads so that they can hide their bodies underwater while looking for prey on the water's surface. Beware! If you see a couple of bumps in the water, an alligator or crocodile might be watching you!

Crocodilians are carnivores—meat eaters. They eat turtles, frogs, birds, fish, and many other kinds of animals that live along the shoreline. Crocodilians don't chew their food— they eat it in chunks. Or, if it's small enough, they eat it whole. If you see an alligator or crocodile jiggling its head around, it's probably trying to swallow a meal.

Baby crocodilians are hatched from eggs that their mothers, or cows, lay in nests along the shore. Most reptiles do not care for their young. But cows are very protective mothers. They guard their eggs. And once the baby crocodilians have hatched, their mothers stay with them until they can live on their own.

Crocodilians' bodies help them to blend in with their surroundings. An alligator or crocodile might look to you like a floating log. Much of the time, crocodilians stay very still. But don't think they're lazy! They can swim up to 20 miles per hour and run up to 11 miles per hour over short distances on land. You don't want to be in a crocodile's way if it's hungry.

The next time you're in Florida, keep your eyes open for alligators and crocodiles. And if you come across one, stay away! These animals are best appreciated from afar.

15 The author gives information in this article by using

    A compare and contrast

    B sequence of events

    C description

    D a summary of ideas

> **Tip:** Articles may be organized in a variety of ways. As you read an article like this one, pay attention to how information is presented to you. Decide whether the author compares two or more things, tells events in order, gives a descriptive list, or provides a general summary.

16 The author tries to persuade the reader that alligators commonly move from one body of fresh water to another by

    F explaining that alligators prefer fresh water

    G describing how alligators hide their bodies under water

    H comparing alligators' "sense organs" to those of crocodiles

    J saying that alligators have been found and seen in odd places

> **Tip:** Authors often try to persuade readers by using convincing language. As you read, look for places where you think the author is trying to back up his or her main points with extra information.

17 According to this article, why does the author think people should stay away from alligators and crocodiles?

    A They eat people more than any other food.

    B They might mistake a person for a log in the water.

    C They can move more quickly than people might expect.

    D They have excellent hearing and might hear a person from far away.

> **Tip:** To find details in an article, identify key words in the question and skim the article for those words. Choose the answer that best explains why people should stay away from alligators and crocodiles.

18 Read this sentence from the article:

If you look closely, you can see that the teeth on the upper and lower jaws of a crocodile interlock like puzzle pieces.

In this sentence, what does the word *interlock* mean?

    F link

    G rub

    H spill

    J carry

> **Tip:** When you come across a word you don't know in a sentence, look for words in surrounding sentences that you do know. Then reread the sentence to see if the other words help you determine the word's meaning.

New York State English Language Arts Standards
15. (1) **Read for information and understanding.** Use knowledge of structure, content, and vocabulary to understand informational text.
16. (3) **Read for critical analysis and evaluation.** Identify author's techniques.
17. (1) **Read for information and understanding.** Draw conclusions and make inferences.
18. (1) **Read for information and understanding.** Use text to understand vocabulary.

19 Which of the following is true about alligators?

- **A** They prefer to live in fresh water.
- **B** Their snouts are pointier than crocodiles' snouts.
- **C** They have "sense organs" all over their body.
- **D** Their teeth are visible when their mouth is closed.

Tip: A true statement will be supported by facts in an article. Review the article to find the statement that can be supported.

20 Alligators and crocodiles have all of these in common EXCEPT

- **F** they are carnivores
- **G** they hatch from eggs
- **H** they have excellent hearing
- **J** they live in the same habitat

Tip: When asked to compare and contrast, draw a chart to list how alligators and crocodiles are alike and different. Then look for ways that alligators and crocodiles are different.

21 Alligators' snouts are designed to be strong because

- **A** it allows them to catch fish more easily
- **B** it allows them to crack shells of animals they eat
- **C** it helps them clean salt out of the water they live in
- **D** it tells them when the pressure of the water has changed

Tip: Scan the article to find important details. Look for the section of the article that tells about alligators' snouts. Read the sentences in this section to figure out why their snouts are strong.

New York State English Language Arts Standards
19. (1) **Read for information and understanding.** Understand stated information.
20. (1) **Read for information and understanding.** Compare and contrast information.
21. (1) **Read for information and understanding.** Understand stated information.

22 What is special about the crocodile's fourth tooth on its lower jaw?

    F It contains sense organs.

    G It arcs upward like a fang.

    H It cleans salt out of the water.

    J It is hidden when the mouth is closed.

> **Tip:** Use clue words from a question to help you find the answer in the article. Scan the article to find where it mentions the crocodile's teeth. Reread this paragraph carefully to figure out what is special about the crocodile's fourth tooth.

23 Based on the article, you would be least likely to find an alligator

    A in a canal

    B in a pond

    C in brackish water

    D in a swimming pool

> **Tip:** Use relevant information from the article to answer the question. Reread the section about where alligators and crocodiles live. Figure out what kind of areas alligators prefer to live in.

24 Crocodilians have eyes on the top of their heads because

    F it measures the pressure of the water

    G it allows them to look like a floating log

    H it lets them look above the surface of the water

    J it makes it easier for them to care for their young

> **Tip:** Articles include details to help explain ideas. Scan the article to find information about crocodilians' eyes. Search for a detail that explains why their eyes are on the top of their heads.

New York State English Language Arts Standards
22. (1) **Read for information and understanding.** Understand stated information.
23. (1) **Listen for information and understanding.** Draw conclusions and make inferences.
24. (1) **Listen for information and understanding.** Understand stated information.

25 How do alligators and crocodiles eat their food? Use details from the article to support your answer.

_____

_____

_____

_____

_____

_____

_____

> **Tip:** When asked to describe how something acts, look for information from the article to help you. Find the part of the article that tells about crocodilians' eating habits. Use a list to organize the details you find.

New York State English Language Arts Standards
25. (1) Read and write for information and understanding. Understand stated information.

Read this excerpt from *The Call of the Wild.* **Then do Numbers 26 through 36.**

The Call of the Wild

by Jack London

Buck lived at a big house in the sun-kissed Santa Clara Valley. Judge Miller's place, as it was called. It stood back from the road, half hidden among the trees, through which glimpses could be caught of the wide cool veranda that ran around its four sides. The house was approached by graveled driveways which wound about through wide-spreading lawns and under the interlacing boughs of tall poplars. At the rear things were on an even more spacious scale than at the front. There were great stables, where a dozen grooms and boys held forth, rows of vine-clad servants' cottages, an endless and orderly array of outhouses, long grape arbors, green pastures, orchards, and berry patches. Then there was the pumping plant for the well, and the big cement tank where Judge Miller's boys took their morning plunge and kept cool in the hot afternoon.

obscurely = distantly

And over this Buck ruled. Here he was born, and here he had lived the four years of his life. It was true, there were other dogs, there could not but be other dogs on so vast a place, but they did not count. They came and went, resided in the populous kennels, or lived obscurely in the recesses of the house after the fashion of Toots, the Japanese pug, or Ysabel, the Mexican hairless—strange creatures that rarely put nose out of doors or set foot to ground. On the other hand, there were the fox terriers, a score of them at least, who yelped fearful promises at Toots and Ysabel looking out of the windows at them and protected by a legion of housemaids armed with brooms and mops.

realm = area

But Buck was neither house-dog nor kennel-dog. The whole realm was his. He plunged into the swimming tank or went hunting with the Judge's sons; he escorted Mollie and Alice, the Judge's daughters, on long twilight or early morning rambles; on wintry nights he lay at the Judge's feet before the roaring library fire; he carried the Judge's grandsons on his back, or rolled them in the grass, and guarded their footsteps through wild adventures down to the fountain in the stable yard, and even beyond. Among the terriers he stalked, and Toots and Ysabel he utterly ignored, for he was king—king over all creeping, crawling, flying things of Judge Miller's place, humans included.

His father, Elmo, a huge St. Bernard, had been the Judge's inseparable companion, and Buck bid fair to follow in the way of his father. He was not so large—he weighed only one hundred and forty pounds—for his mother, Shep, had been a Scotch shepherd dog. Nevertheless, one hundred and forty pounds, to which was added the dignity that comes of good living and universal respect, enabled him to carry himself in right royal fashion. He had a fine pride in himself, was even a trifle egotistical, as country gentlemen sometimes become because of their situation. But he had saved himself by not becoming a mere pampered house-dog. Hunting and kindred outdoor delights had kept down the fat and hardened his muscles; and to him, as to the cold-tubbing races, the love of water had been a tonic and health preserver.

26 Which of the following best describes Buck?

    F lazy

    G timid

    H conceited

    J hostile

> **Tip:** When asked to describe a character, think about how the character acts in the story. Reread the story and figure out how the author describes Buck's attitude.

27 In the story, the author compares Buck to a

    A strange creature

    B country gentleman

    C small horse

    D kennel dog

> **Tip:** Authors sometimes compare a character to someone or something else. Look through the story to find an example of a comparison involving Buck.

28 Buck wants to be the Judge's "inseparable companion" to

    F spend more time in the house

    G prove that he is better than other dogs

    H keep from living in the kennel

    J follow in his father's footsteps

> **Tip:** Understand what makes a character do certain things by skimming the story for an explanation. Look for the words "inseparable companion" in the story. Look at the nearby sentences to find out why Buck wants to do what his father did.

New York State English Language Arts Standards
26. (2) **Read for literary response and expression.** Interpret characters.
27. (2) **Read for literary response and expression.** Determine use of a literary device.
28. (2) **Read for literary response and expression.** Interpret characters.

29 Which of the following words means the same as *pampered*?

- A spoiled
- B enjoyed
- C bored
- D ignored

> **Tip:** To figure out the meaning of a word, look at how it fits into the sentence. Buck is glad he has not become "a mere pampered house-dog." Look at the four answer choices, and decide which one of them best fits the context of the sentence.

30 How do you know that this story is fiction?

- F It takes place in the past.
- G It describes the character's thoughts.
- H It contains dialogue and a plot.
- J It gives information about the setting.

> **Tip:** Fiction has certain features that make it different from nonfiction. Nonfiction is about events that actually happened, but fiction includes made-up events. Think about which of these could only happen in a fiction story.

31 This story is told by a

- A first person narrator
- B second person narrator
- C third person limited narrator
- D third person omniscient narrator

> **Tip:** Remember that most stories have either a first person or third person narrator. If the narrator uses the pronoun "I" to write about himself or herself, the story is an example of first person narration. If it is the third person, decide whether the narrator describes the thoughts of several different characters or just one character.

32 Read this excerpt from the passage:

They came and went, resided in the populous kennels, or lived obscurely in the recesses of the house...

As it is used above, the word *populous* means

- F dirty
- G crowded
- H brand-new
- J underground

> **Tip:** A good way to figure out the meaning of a word you don't know is to look at the words around it. The sentence states that many dogs lived in the kennels. With that knowledge, you can decide which of these answer choices is the best definition of *populous*.

New York State English Language Arts Standards
29. (2) **Read for literary response and expression.** Use context to determine meaning.
30. (3) **Read for critical analysis and evaluation.** Identify author's purpose.
31. (2) **Read for literary response and expression.** Identify author's point of view.
32. (2) **Read for literary response and expression.** Use context to determine meaning.

33 Buck does all of the following EXCEPT

    A go swimming with the Judge's sons

    B play games with Toots and Ysabel

    C lie at the Judge's feet next to the fire

    D take walks with the Judge's daughters

Tip: Stories often include details about what characters do. Reread the story, and look for a description of Buck's actions. Decide which of the four choices is not mentioned as one of his activities.

34 Which of these is true about Buck?

    F His mother was a St. Bernard.

    G He lives in the Santa Clara Valley.

    H His father was a Scotch shepherd dog.

    J He weighs over two hundred pounds.

Tip: Read a story carefully to recall important details. Look at each of the four answer choices and see if it is supported by details in the story. Only one of them will be supported.

35 Why does Buck enjoy hunting?

    A It is easy to do.

    B It protects the house.

    C It makes him stronger.

    D It provides him with food.

Tip: In a story, ideas are usually supported with relevant details. Scan the story and find where it tells about hunting. Read through the paragraph to decide why Buck enjoys hunting.

New York State English Language Arts Standards
33. (2) Read for literary response and expression. Interpret plot.
34. (2) Read for literary response and expression. Interpret characters.
35. (2) Read for literary response and expression. Interpret characters.

36 From the way the author describe Buck's house, what do you think it looks like? Use details from the story to support your answer.

_____

_____

_____

_____

_____

_____

_____

> **Tip:** Authors often use descriptive language to tell about the setting of a story. Read the story again, and look for words and phrases that describe Buck's surroundings.

Read the following story about a family's sacrifice to help one of their own. Then do Numbers 37 through 43.

The Sacrifice

"Eduardo, are you still with us?" Eduardo jerked awake, furious with himself for falling asleep again in Ms. Browning's algebra class. She was an exceptional teacher and he loved math. But he was exhausted, with every cell in his brain demanding sleep.

After class, Ms. Browning stopped him. "Eduardo, what's going on? You're a great student, but you seem so tired recently. Maybe you should watch less TV."

Eduardo nodded and left for his next class. He thought to himself, "Less TV? I never have time to watch TV."

Eduardo was exhausted when he worked at Dan's Hamburgers that evening. His manager pulled him aside to go over all the mistakes he made. Eduardo knew his job backward and forward, but his listless brain had betrayed him.

He got home at nine o'clock and found his sister Amalia doing homework at the computer, yawning.

"Where's Norma?" he asked. His oldest sister was usually home by this time.

"She and Papá are both working overtime." Amalia looked up and asked quietly, "Do you ever resent what all of us have to do so Manuel can be a doctor one day?"

Eduardo didn't answer. Throughout the day, he'd thought about his brother Manuel living in a town far away from home, doing no more work than keeping up his grades. The worst part was that Manuel was only in his second year at the university. After that there was still medical school.

In the morning, Eduardo woke up with a start, his heart pounding. He was grateful to be rescued from his dream.

The dream had been so real. He and Manuel were at a swimming pool. As Eduardo was paddling around, his brother jumped off the high diving board. Suddenly, an enormous weight crashed on top of Eduardo. He tried with all his strength to push off Manuel, but his brother stayed frozen in the position of his dive, unaware that there was anything underneath him. Eduardo, flailing his arms, came to the end of his breath in the very moment he heard the alarm clock.

Eduardo sat down at the kitchen table with his mother. "My son, do you feel well?" she asked him. "Twice last night I heard you moaning in your sleep. In fact, lately your sleep is often restless. You're too young for that. Tell me what's troubling you."

Eduardo saw the worry in his mother's eyes. "It's just that ... I feel exhausted all the time," he told her. "I'm too tired to do well at school like I used to. I'm tired when I'm working at Dan's. I'm tired when I mow lawns on the weekend. I'm even too tired to sleep well. And I feel guilty because I know all of us are working so Manuel can be a doctor one day."

"How difficult this must be for you," his mother sighed, stroking his hands. "You never complained about the plan your father and I proposed—that each of us contributes to help Manuel get an education and eventually he will help you and your sisters."

His mother paused. She was gazing beyond him, her thoughts as distant as a far-off star.

"Extremely difficult," she repeated. "What we're doing for Manuel, as a family, is very common among the people we left behind in Nicaragua. But it's not quite as common, I think, among the people of this adopted country of ours."

"Growing up in the United States, you don't know the old ways. This makes coping even harder for you. And I don't want your schoolwork to suffer. We'll have to do something about that. Oh, my dear, dear son." His mother's face was creased with concern.

Eduardo squeezed his mother's hand and said, "Don't worry, Mamá." He'd just realized that he felt a little lighter, a little less burdened. "We'll work things out together, as a family."

He stood up to gather his books. "Now it's time for me to leave. I don't want to be late for school."

37 Which of the following sentences best summarizes the first three paragraphs?

  A Ms. Browning mistakenly thinks Eduardo watches too much TV.

  B Math has always been Eduardo's favorite subject.

  C Eduardo is too tired to stay alert in math class.

  D Eduardo is upset about not being able to watch TV.

Tip: To summarize a certain part of a story, think about what you learned by reading it. Reread the first three paragraphs. Decide what they are all mainly about.

38 Read this sentence from the passage:

Eduardo knew his job backward and forward, but his listless brain had betrayed him.

In this sentence, what does *listless* mean?

  F eager

  G young

  H damaged

  J tired

Tip: When you need to find the meaning of a word, consider how it fits into the sentence. Think about what would cause Eduardo to make so many mistakes. Decide which word would mean the same as *listless*.

39 When Amalia asks Eduardo if he ever resents what he has to do to help his brother, Eduardo does not answer because

  A he still has things to do before going to bed

  B he wants to keep his true feelings to himself

  C he is too busy thinking about his brother

  D he is exhausted from having worked all day

Tip: When you want to understand a character's feelings, skim the story to find examples of issues that make that character feel a certain way. Find the part of the story in which Amalia asks Eduardo this question. Check the sentences near it to figure out how Eduardo is feeling at the time.

New York State English Language Arts Standards
37. (2) **Read for literary response and expression.** Interpret theme.
38. (2) **Read ford literary response and expression.** Use context to determine meaning.
39. (2) **Read for literary response and expression.** Interpret characters.

40 The author writes that Eduardo's mother "was gazing beyond him, her thoughts as distant as a far-off star" to show that she is

- **F** thinking of what life was like in Nicaragua
- **G** worrying about Manuel at college, living far away from home
- **H** regretting that she ever moved to the United States
- **J** trying to figure out Eduardo's words

Tip: Authors use descriptive language to help the reader understand important ideas. This quotation indicates that Eduardo's mother is thinking about something that happened long ago. Decide which answer best fits this idea.

41 Eduardo's mother realizes that because her son did not grow up in Nicaragua, it is harder for him to

- **A** do well in his subjects in school
- **B** appreciate the differences between Nicaragua and the United States
- **C** learn how to set goals and meet them
- **D** understand personal sacrifice for a family goal

Tip: Important ideas in a story are supported by details. Reread Eduardo's mother's speech to her son at the end of the story. Look closely to see what she thinks is hard for Eduardo.

42 From the events in the story, the reader can conclude that the story takes place

- **F** at the present time in a city in Nicaragua
- **G** about sixty years ago in a small town in the United States
- **H** about sixty years ago in a small town in Nicaragua
- **J** at the present time in a city in the United States

Tip: When a question asks you about setting, look for key details in the story. This story gives clues about the time period in which the story takes place, such as the references to television and computers.

43 When Eduardo's mother says, "Oh, my dear, dear son," the author creates a mood of

- **A** tenderness
- **B** bitterness
- **C** irony
- **D** lightheartedness

Tip: An author uses certain language to convey a mood or feeling in a story. Find the paragraph that includes the phrase, "Oh, my dear, dear son." Look at the kind of tone the author expresses. Think about what Eduardo's mother says and does in this paragraph, and decide how she is feeling at the time.

New York State English Language Arts Standards
40. (2) **Read for literary response and expression.** Recognize how author's language use creates feelings.
41. (2) **Read for literary response and expression.** Interpret plot.
42. (2) **Read for literary response and expression.** Interpret setting.
43. (2) **Read for literary response and expression.** Recognize how author's language use creates feelings.

NYS Modeled Instruction: Listening

DIRECTIONS: In this section, you will listen to the article "Sequoyah." Then you will answer some questions to show how well you understood what was read.

You will listen to the story twice. As you listen carefully, you may take notes on the story anytime you wish during the readings. You may use these notes to answer the questions that follow.

> **Tip:** Listen carefully for main ideas and details. In your notes, answer the questions *who, what, when, where, why,* and *how.* Focus on key ideas and descriptive words and phrases rather than complete sentences.

Notes

1 According to the article, what is a syllabary?

   A small drawings that look like letters of the alphabet

   B an alphabet that orders letters and symbols in a sequence

   C a system of pictures that represents actions in a language

   D a set of symbols that represent each spoken sound or syllable

> **Tip:** When you are trying to find information about a difficult word, use clues that come from the word itself as well as other information in the text. Put these clues together to find the answer.

2 Sequoyah's syllabary was a success because

   F it made language with pictographs easy to learn

   G it prevented the downfall of his people

   H it was immediately accepted by all the Cherokee people

   J it allowed the Cherokee to read and write in their own language

> **Tip:** Authors often support their ideas with details. Review information about the syllabary. Look for the details that support the idea that Sequoyah's syllabary was a success.

3 Sequoyah's hunting injury was not serious because

   A he had more time for study after the injury

   B he could not travel very far after the injury

   C he served as a soldier after the injury

   D he needed his daughter's help after the injury

> **Tip:** When you draw a conclusion from a story, you should be able to support it with information from the story. Look in your notes for information about Sequoyah's hunting accident. Then decide which statement will help you understand the seriousness of his hunting accident.

4 Read this sentence from the passage:

   In some instances, settlers and tribes lived in peace with each other, but before long the settlers' demands for land began to push the Cherokee and Creek out of their ancestral homes.

   In this sentence, what does *ancestral* mean?

   F ancient and unused

   G belonging to one's family from old times

   H belonging to one's parents

   J no longer owned

> **Tip:** Sometimes you can use what you already know about a word to understand an unfamiliar word. For example, the word *ancestral* looks similar to the word *ancestor*. The two words have the same root. Use what you already know about the meaning of *ancestor* to figure out which meaning is correct.

New York State English Language Arts Standards
1. **(1) Listen for information and understanding.** Use knowledge of structure, content, and vocabulary to understand informational text.
2. **(1) Listen for information and understanding.** Draw conclusions and make inferences.
3. **(1) Listen for information and understanding.** Draw conclusions and make inferences.
4. **(1) Listen for information and understanding.** Use text to understand vocabulary.

5 Why was the syllabary so important to the Cherokee people? Use details from the story to support your answer.

_____

_____

_____

_____

_____

_____

_____

> **Tip:** When you are trying to find the main reason something happened, you may have to look outside the story to find the answer. Think about how your ability to write helps yourself and others. Decide which of these ways are most important to your life and culture. Then relate your thoughts to the Cherokee people and what the syllabary did for them.

New York State English Language Arts Standards
5. (3) Listen and write for critical analysis and evaluation. Use critical analysis to evaluate information.

6 How do you know that Sequoyah was determined to finish his syllabary? Use information from the story in your answer.

_____

_____

_____

_____

_____

_____

> **Tip:** Usually you can figure out how a person feels based on his or her actions. Think about how Sequoyah acted as he worked on his syllabary. Give examples of how he continued to work hard despite some setbacks. This will show why he is determined.

New York State English Language Arts Standards
6. (1) **Listen and write for information and understanding.** Draw conclusions and make inferences.

NYS Modeled Instruction: Writing

DIRECTIONS: In this section, you will find and correct mistakes in a paragraph. The mistakes will be with capitalization, punctuation, and grammar.

Practice Task

> I love going to baseball games the field is so big and, the players are really good. They get better every time I see them. There are so many homeruns and. Great plays. My dad buys me a peanuts and soda. It is so much fun to watch the crowd do wild when the home team wins. I wish I could go to the ballpark every day.

Editing Task

> **Read the paragraph and draw a line through each mistake. Write the correction above the mistake. Not all the sentences have mistakes. There are no misspelled words.**
>
> I broke my arm last week. It started when I saw my dog, biff, chewing on my homework. Biff loved the taste of that homework for some reason. I try to pull the homework out of his mouth, but Biff was stubborn and won't release it. Suddenly, Biff yanked on my arm, who pulled me off balance. I fall over backward and broke my arm. Next time Biff eats my homework, I won't struggle with him.

> 🌀 **Tip:** When you write, make sure that you end each sentence with a period or a question mark. Also, use capital letters only for proper names and for the first word of a sentence. Finally, make sure that the grammar is accurate. For example, remember to write in complete sentences and use correct verb tenses.

New York State English Language Arts Standards
(1) **Write for information and understanding.** Use punctuation and capitalization correctly.
(1) **Write for information and understanding.** Use correct grammatical construction.

NYS Testing Program Test-Taking Tips

Now you are ready to take a Practice Test for the New York State English Language Arts Test. Use what you learned in the Modeled Instruction section of this book to help you do well on the test. Remember these hints when you are taking the test.

Remember these tips when you are taking the test.

- **Listen** carefully to the directions. Be sure to read all of the directions in the Practice Test section. Ask your teacher to explain any directions you do not understand.

- **Read** each passage carefully. Then read each question carefully. As you answer the questions, you may look back at the reading selections as often as you like.

- **Listen** carefully when a passage is read to you. Try to imagine the setting, characters, and action of the story as you listen. Take notes that will help you answer the questions after you have heard the story. Look back at your notes as often as you like when you answer questions about the story.

- **Look over** the paragraph you are editing to find and correct all mistakes.

- When you take the Practice Test, you will answer multiple-choice questions on a separate Answer Sheet. Fill in the answer bubbles completely. If you change your answer, be sure to erase your first answer completely.

- When you answer the short-response questions, be sure to include details from the reading or listening selections to support your answers. You will write your answers in this book in the spaces provided.

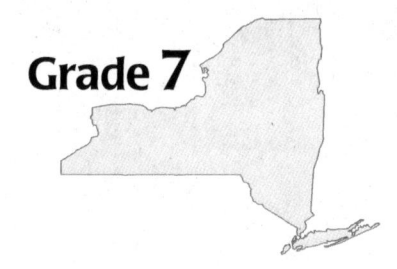

New York State Testing Program

Grade 7

English Language Arts Practice Test

Book 1

Name _____

Session 1

Directions

Read the following story about a fishing trip that turns into a mystery. Then do Numbers 1 through 8.

The Thousand Islands Mystery

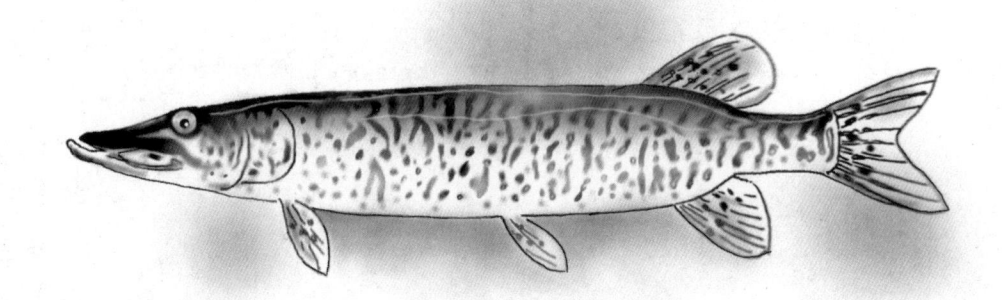

We were going to the Thousand Islands for the weekend! I'd been nagging my dad forever to take me fishing there, because I love fishing more than anything else. I was as happy as a clam. I even planned out which boat we would take: the *Reel Deal*, a 27-footer, equipped with great technology like radar and sonar. I packed up my clothes, sunscreen, drinks, and a cooler.

On Saturday morning, my dad and I clambered into the *Reel Deal*. We were greeted by the boat's captain, Mike. We set sail for Wellesley Island with Captain Mike at the controls. I asked if I could use the radar and sonar to look for some fish. Mike showed me how.

Then he told me to look for an old shipwreck called the *Roy A. Jodrey* that had sunk in 1974. I knew that fish loved to gather around shipwrecks, so I started scanning for the *Jodrey*. Within minutes, the radar was pinging loudly as we approached the wreck.

The weird thing was that there were no fish around the *Jodrey*. I checked the sonar. There definitely were no muskellunge, walleye, northern pike, or bass swimming around. There wasn't even a single minnow.

Go On

Captain Mike urged us to try better fishing waters. Dad was anxious to move on, too. But I insisted we stay. I just kept scanning with the sonar. Something wasn't right about this. I was sure that fish should be swimming around the *Jodrey's* mast, but there weren't any. Then I noticed that a bulge near the ship was showing up on the screen. I held my breath, hoping it was a huge muskellunge. But as the seconds passed by, the bulge didn't move. Fish usually didn't stay still.

I showed Captain Mike the mysterious reading on the screen. Mike took more readings and said that the bulge most likely was made of metal. He used the radio to call his friend, Barbara, who was the captain of a nearby Coast Guard boat. Captain Barbara asked us some questions. She agreed that it was very abnormal to have an old wreck that wasn't surrounded by fish. She said her dive team wanted to check out this weird metal bulge.

When the Coast Guard boat arrived, I gave them the coordinates of the bulge. Three divers suited up and plopped into the water. After a while, the divers came back up. They had found a pile of eight old barrels that must have fallen from the *Jodrey*. The barrels were slowly leaking oil into the water. There were no fish because the water was polluted!

The Coast Guard captain thanked us for alerting them to the problem. Barbara said I would probably get a reward for helping them. She said I would make a good member of the Coast Guard someday. Then Mike, Dad, and I had to leave the area so the water could be cleaned.

Captain Mike said he knew where we could find some fish, so we headed out. We ended up catching many big fish that afternoon. I had a fun day of fishing and I helped solve a mystery, all in one day!

1 Read this sentence from the passage.

She agreed that it was very abnormal to have an old wreck that wasn't surrounded by fish.

In this sentence, what does *abnormal* mean?

- **A** usual
- **B** strange
- **C** healthy
- **D** pleasant

2 This story is told by a

- **F** first person narrator
- **G** second person narrator
- **H** third person limited narrator
- **J** third person omniscient narrator

3 All of these are true about the *Reel Deal* EXCEPT

- **A** it is 27 feet long
- **B** it carries oil barrels
- **C** it has radar and sonar
- **D** it is captained by Mike

4 Which excerpt from the story uses a simile, the literary technique that compares two things?

- **F** I was as happy as a clam.
- **G** But as the seconds passed by, the bulge didn't move.
- **H** Three divers suited up and plopped into the water.
- **J** Within minutes, the radar was pinging loudly as we approached the wreck.

Go On

Session 1 NYS Testing Program Practice Test • 37

5 How does the narrator know something is wrong at the shipwreck site?

    A The sonar is not working correctly.

    B He notices that the water is polluted.

    C There are no fish anywhere near the wreck.

    D He can smell the oil leak from the barrels.

6 The author gives information in this story by using

    F sequence

    G cause and effect

    H compare and contrast

    J order of importance

7 The main purpose of "The Thousand Islands Mystery" is to

    A tell an entertaining story

    B persuade readers to go fishing

    C warn about the dangers of pollution

    D inform readers about different types of fish

Go On

8 How is the mystery of the metal bulge solved? Use details from the story to explain your answer.

Directions

Read this story about constellations and Greek myths. Then do Numbers 9 through 15.

Star Stories

On a clear night you can see many stars in the sky, especially if you are out in the country. The stars shine brilliantly down upon the earth. Stargazing is a favorite hobby of many people all around the world.

Some stars are grouped into patterns called constellations. There are many different constellations. Some familiar constellations, like the Big Dipper, are visible all year. Others, though, can only be seen during certain times of the year. They come and go with the seasons.

Constellations have interesting names. Some are named after animals, such as Ursa Major (Great Bear), Cancer (Crab), Capricorn (Goat), Aries (Ram), Taurus (Bull), and Pisces (Fish). Other constellations are named after people from Greek myths.

Ancient stories describe many of these constellations. Two stories that come from Greek myths tell about the winter constellations of Cassiopeia, the queen, and Orion, the hunter. The first is a story of pride while the second is a story of tragedy.

Long ago, there was a queen in Ethiopia named Cassiopeia. She was quite beautiful and had given birth to a daughter, Andromeda, who grew up to be as beautiful as the queen herself. Cassiopeia, though, was very selfish. She was not content with the gifts of beauty, power, and motherhood that the gods had granted her. Cassiopeia wanted more. She wanted to be called the most beautiful woman. She boasted that she was more beautiful than the daughters of the gods. Her bragging made the gods very angry.

Again and again in Greek stories, the gods punish mortals who are too proud, and Cassiopeia was no exception. The divine immortals transported the vain queen to the stars,

Go On

where she is chained forever to her throne. To further humble her, they decreed that she must hang her head down in the sky at times. She remains in that spot to this very day. You can see the Cassiopeia constellation all year long because it rotates around the North Star.

The myth of Orion tells of a man who was placed among the stars as an honor, not as a punishment. Orion was a mighty Greek hunter whose father was rumored to be a god of the sea. No prey could escape Orion's bow, and the gods praised his skills. One creature did escape Orion, however—a lovely princess. He fell in love with her, and she with him. But her father, the king, disliked Orion and wanted to prevent the marriage. He ordered a servant to blind Orion, so that the princess would not love him.

The king's wicked plan worked. After Orion became blind, the princess denied his love. Even worse, Orion could no longer hunt. The gods felt sorry for him, so they sent a messenger who told him to face the rising sun and reclaim his sight.

Despite the gods' favor, Orion met a tragic fate. While pursuing an animal across a field one day, Orion stepped on a scorpion. His foot crushed it, but its sting killed the hunter. In pity, the gods placed Orion in the sky, with his hunting dogs and some of his prey—the bear and the rabbit. Orion strides across the winter sky, holding out his bow, reaching for an arrow. His shoulders form a triangle of stars. Three bright stars make up the sword that hangs from his belt, as he hunts forever in the night sky. His enemy the scorpion is also in the sky, but since that constellation only rises in the summer, the two are never seen in the sky together.

Orion, Cassiopeia, and all the other constellations still light up the night sky. The next time you go stargazing, you will know where these bright pictures in the sky came from.

9 Read this sentence from the passage:

The divine immortals transported the vain queen to the stars, where she is chained forever to her throne.

In this sentence, what does *immortals* mean?

- **A** strong men
- **B** beautiful women
- **C** frightening aliens
- **D** undying beings

10 Which of the following is an opinion?

- **F** Constellations are patterns of stars.
- **G** Cassiopeia's punishment was cruel and unfair.
- **H** Many star stories come from ancient myths.
- **J** Orion and Cassiopeia are constellations of the winter sky.

11 What was probably the author's purpose in writing this passage?

- **A** to amuse readers with a funny story about the gods
- **B** to inform readers about myths that explain certain star patterns
- **C** to persuade readers to create their own stories about constellations
- **D** to warn readers about the consequences of being too proud or too much in love

12 In the story of Orion, which of these events happened first?

- **F** Orion stepped on a scorpion.
- **G** Orion fell in love with a princess.
- **H** The king ordered a servant to blind Orion.
- **J** A messenger told Orion to face the rising run.

13 The Cassiopeia constellation is visible all year long because

　A it rises in the summer
　B it consists of many bright stars
　C it rotates around the North Star
　D Cassiopeia is chained to her throne

14 Which of the following words means the same as *humble*?

　F impress
　G disgrace
　H honor
　J understand

15 All of the following are true EXCEPT

　A the Big Dipper is visible all year
　B many stars are visible on a clear night
　C the scorpion is a summer constellation
　D the Orion constellation can be seen all year long

Go On

Directions

Read this article about Louis Braille, inventor of a reading and writing system for the blind. Then do Numbers 16 through 21.

Louis Braille: Hope for the Blind

Louis Braille, the inventor of a reading and writing system for the blind, was born in Coupvray, France, in 1809. He was the fourth child of a leather worker. One day when Louis was three years old, he injured his eye while playing with a sharp tool from his father's workbench.

Unfortunately, Louis was not treated by a doctor. Instead, an elderly woman from the village tried to treat his eye with home remedies, but the eye soon became infected. When the infection spread to Louis's other eye, he became blind. It was a tragic accident that would challenge Louis's intellect and creativity throughout his life.

With determination, Louis Braille refused to let his blindness set the course of his life as it might have done for many others during that time. Louis Braille was intelligent and creative. He was lucky to be befriended by a priest, Jacques Palluy, and a schoolteacher, Antoine Becheret. These two men arranged for Louis to go to school in the village where Louis could learn by listening instead of reading.

Despite his blindness, Louis was soon at the head of his class. His hard work earned him a scholarship to the Royal Institute for Blind Youth in Paris when he was only ten years old. But Louis still was not able to read and write.

As the youngest child in the school, Louis was often teased by his classmates. However, he did very well at school, learning his academic subjects with the help of leather books printed with large, raised letters.

While he was at the school, another important figure entered Louis Braille's life. Charles Barbier de la Serre was a clever nobleman who had escaped death at the hands of the mob during the French Revolution. As a soldier, he had invented a secret code of writing that could be read in the dark by touch. That way, a soldier's position would not be given away by the sound of his voice when he passed along a message.

The code was based on dots and dashes. Barbier called his system of communication "sonography" because it wasn't based on the actual spelling of words, but on their sounds. He was convinced that the system could be used to help the blind learn to read. The school director allowed students to experiment with the dots and dashes of the code. The moment Louis touched the raised figures, he knew something wonderful had happened.

Go On

Louis improved upon the Barbier system, making it less cumbersome by reducing Barbier's twelve-dot cell to only six dots and a few dashes. It took Louis about three years to solve the problems, but he was dedicated to making the system work.

| cumbersome = awkward |

The other students at the Royal Institute of Blind Youth loved his new system. But the school's teachers did not welcome the task of learning it for themselves. They all had normal sight and felt no urgency to learn another system of writing.

For the next two years, Louis continued to develop his skills. He became the first blind apprentice teacher at the school when he was only seventeen. He also found work as a church organist. In 1828, he had combined his interests in Braille with his love of music to come up with a way to copy music using his new system of writing. His book, *Method of Writing Words, Music, and Plain Songs by means of Dots, for use by the Blind and Arranged for Them,* was published in 1829. Louis Braille was just twenty years old.

Louis soon became one of the first blind professors at the school. His students considered him a wonderful teacher who helped them in many ways. His successes eventually inspired other professors to begin using Louis Braille's alphabet to teach their students.

Conditions in the school were crowded and unsanitary, and Louis contracted tuberculosis in the cold, dank school building. But he wouldn't let that slow him down. Louis Braille continued to teach and work on improving his system of writing. He also invented raphigraphy, an alphabet made of large print letters in dots, so that students could write letters to family members.

In 1834, Louis Braille showed his work at the Paris Exhibition of Industry. Word of the new system began to spread like wildfire throughout France. People began to realize that the blind would be more independent if they had a way to communicate.

Louis Braille would not live to see his work become popular. He died in 1852, two years before France made Braille the official reading and writing system for the blind.

Today, after more than 150 years, blind students continue to use the Braille system to read. The system continues to use the basic six-dot model, and teachers are more skilled at helping blind students learn to use the system effectively. Teachers say that with proper teaching, a blind child using Louis Braille's system can learn to read at about the same speed as a sighted child when both children begin learning to read at about the same age.

Braille signs are posted in elevators. Braille books are available to blind students around the world. Louis Braille overcame the challenges of his blindness and poor health to help generations of blind children meet the challenge of living without sight in a sighted world.

Go On

16 The author gives information in this article by using

    F compare and contrast

    G cause and effect

    H sequence

    J order of importance

17 Which detail supports the idea that Louis Braille overcame difficult challenges?

    A Braille became blind from an accident as a child.

    B Students at the Royal Institute of Blind Youth loved Braille's system.

    C Braille created a system that let blind people read and write.

    D Students still use the Braille system today to learn to read.

18 According to the story, Louis Braille was challenged by both his blindness and

    F conflicting feelings about leaving home to attend school in Paris

    G crowded, unsanitary conditions at the Paris school

    H unfriendly teachers who did not want him in their classes

    J his parents' lack of interest in education for the blind

Go On

19 From the information in the story, the reader can conclude that Louis Braille's blindness was a result of

   A other health problems that were discovered too late

   B the original injury to his eye

   C lack of proper medical treatment

   D unhealthy conditions in his father's workshop

20 Which statement best expresses the main idea of the article?

   F Education is the best way to overcome life's challenges.

   G Mistakes that you make as a child usually affect your whole life.

   H Other people will always be there to help you meet challenges.

   J The best way to meet life's challenges is by not letting setbacks defeat you.

21 The author probably would agree with which statement?

   A Louis Braille would have done better if he had had fewer challenges.

   B Greater challenges always make people give up.

   C Meeting difficult challenges helps make people try harder.

   D Other people were mostly responsible for Louis Braille's success.

Go On

Directions

Read this story about an adopted girl trying to adjust to her new surroundings. Then do Numbers 22 through 28.

Then and Now

Lavinia awoke with the rooster's crow but was reluctant to get out of bed. She didn't want to abandon her dreams, her one link with the loved ones from her past. Just as she was slipping into another dream, she heard Madame's voice reverberating from below. "Girl, shake off that laziness and go milk the cows!" Lavinia sighed, then scrambled out of bed and into her clothes. As she climbed down the ladder that led to the loft where she slept, Madame's scowling face appeared through each space between the rungs.

reverberating = echoing

"Good morning, ma'am," Lavinia mumbled as she took the chunk of bread that Madame held out to her.

"Morning?" Madame replied. "The morning's practically over. Can't you hear those poor cows bellowing in distress? Get to work, girl."

Hero, a big sheepdog, was waiting outside the door for Lavinia. The faithful animal was usually at her side while she did her outdoor chores. On her way to the barn, she ate the bread, except for the last bite, which went to Hero. Before she entered the dark, clammy barn, Lavinia noticed that the rising sun seemed to be on fire.

As she milked one cow after another, she thought idly about the nature of fire. It was beautiful to gaze upon, but its power to destroy was the reason she was now living what she had come to think of as her second life.

Lavinia closed her eyes to focus on the scene from her first life that often played inside her head. She was lying on a rug before the fireplace after supper, finding the shapes of fantasy objects in the embers that surrounded the flames. Her mother sat in a chair nearby, squinting in the dim light to do her needlework. Her father was just outside the cottage, completing his final chores. She felt warm and content, safe and loved.

"That was then and this is now," Lavinia heard someone utter in a gravelly voice. She opened her eyes in amazement and looked around. Besides herself, the cows and Hero were the only

Go On

living creatures in the barn. She got up from the milking stool to look out the door, but no one was there. Behind her, coming from Hero's direction, she heard the same voice again. "What if Madame hadn't taken you in?" She wheeled around to face the dog, whose head was cocked to one side as if he were anticipating an answer.

Lavinia kneeled by the dog and scratched his head. "Hero, are you so wise that you've learned to talk?" she asked skeptically.

While milking the last cow, she thought about the question posed in the gravelly voice. The night her destiny changed, a kind-hearted stranger passing nearby had dared to enter her burning cottage, but he managed to rescue only the little girl from the blaze. At daybreak, the villagers gathered to discuss her fate, since they knew of no kinfolk who could raise her. The only villager who offered to take in young Lavinia was Madame Tarski, a childless widow.

Lavinia often wondered whether Madame ever regretted bringing her home. She had never asked herself what her fate might have been had Madame not stepped forward.

Lavinia carried the full milk pails out the barn door, followed by Hero. "This is now, you say?" she asked, looking at him. Moving her gaze slowly from left to right, she focused on the old but sturdy house she now lived in, then on the apple trees in bloom, then on the fields covered in wildflowers. Next, she noticed that the sun no longer seemed on fire as it climbed through a sky of cornflower blue.

She picked up a stick to throw to Hero. When he enthusiastically returned it, she stroked his thick fur. At that moment Madame called out, "Girl, time to start the bread making."

This time, when Lavinia heard Madame's call, she almost smiled. In a few hours, the wonderful aroma of baking bread would fill the house. Lavinia couldn't wait.

22 The author probably wrote this passage to

　　F persuade people to live on farms
　　G express ideas about country living
　　H tell the biography of Lavinia
　　J entertain readers with a story

23 From the story, the reader can conclude that

　　A humans can learn from animals
　　B misfortune may happen to someone who least expects it
　　C a person lives more fully by appreciating the present
　　D an act of kindness is always appreciated

24 In the story, the author creates a mood that changes from

　　F desperate to joyous
　　G thoughtful to bitter
　　H regretful to hopeful
　　J sad to resentful

25 The author states "she noticed that the sun no longer seemed on fire" to help the reader understand

   A that the sun is rising as the day goes on
   B how Lavinia's life was better in the past
   C that Lavinia is no longer haunted by fire
   D how the sun can change its appearance

26 Read this sentence from the story:

She wheeled around to face the dog, whose head was cocked to one side as if he were anticipating an answer.

In this sentence, the word *anticipating* means

   F watching
   G giving
   H drinking
   J expecting

27 The sixth paragraph of this story is important because it

   A describes a symbol of Lavinia's first life
   B flashes back to Lavinia's earlier life
   C foreshadows what Lavinia's second life will be like
   D changes the story's point of view

28 Why does Lavinia become happier about her new surroundings by the end of the story? Explain what changes her mind, using details from the story to support your answer.

_____

_____

_____

_____

_____

_____

_____

Grade 7

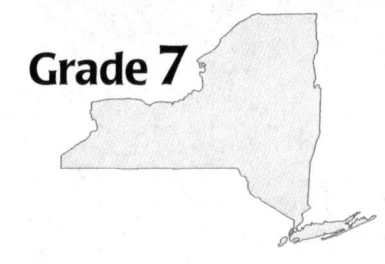

New York State Testing Program

English Language Arts Practice Test

Book 2

Name _____

Session 2

Part 1: Listening

*D*irections

In this part of the test, you will listen to the article "Layers of Protection." Then you will answer some questions to show how well you understood what was read.

You will listen to the article twice. As you listen carefully, you may take notes on the story anytime you wish during the readings. You may use these notes to answer the questions that follow. Use the space on page 55 for your notes.

Go On

Notes

29 Which statement from the article is an opinion?

A Because the atmosphere protects us, we should take care to protect the atmosphere.

B Because no weather occurs in this layer, the air is calm, and jets can cruise easily at the lower edge of the stratosphere, the tropopause.

C We live in the innermost layer, the troposphere, which extends about ten miles above the planet's surface.

D When you watch meteor showers, the streaks of light through the night sky occur in the mesosphere, which keeps all but the largest of chunks of space rock from colliding with the planet.

30 How does the stratosphere protect Earth?

F It is rich in oxygen.

G It burns up meteors.

H It holds water vapor in place.

J It shields Earth from damaging solar rays.

31 Which layer prevents chunks of space rock from colliding with the planet?

- **A** tropopause
- **B** mesosphere
- **C** exosphere
- **D** ionosphere

32 Read this sentence from the article:

The stratosphere also nurtures life on Earth because it contains the ozone layer that protects Earth from ultraviolet rays.

In this sentence, the word *nurtures* means

- **F** harms
- **G** reflects
- **H** supports
- **J** pollutes

33 Why is the Earth's atmosphere important? Use information from the story to explain your answer.

_____
_____
_____
_____
_____
_____
_____

34 In what ways does the troposphere maintain life? Support your answer with details from the story.

Session 2

Part 2: Writing

DIRECTIONS: In this section, you will find and correct mistakes in a paragraph. The mistakes will be with capitalization, punctuation, and grammar.

Practice Task

> I love pizza. Its my favorite food. Every time I go on a trip with my Friends, I make them stop at a pizza place. They are probably sick of pizza by now, but I am not. I like pizza with pepperoni, onions sausage, mushrooms, and anchovies. I would like to own a pizza parlor when I get older, I could eat pizza every day.

Editing Task

Read the paragraph and draw a line through each mistake. Write the correction above the mistake. Not all the sentences have mistakes. There are no misspelled words.

> Yesterday, my brother and I went to the zoo. At first, I was upset that I would have to wake up early, But I find out that the zoo was better than sleeping until noon. When we walk through the entrance gate, the first thing I saw was a huge pool with three grizzly bears swimming in it. After we saw the bears, we spent a few more hours looking at many other animals. We visited the gorillas giraffes, and elephants. I was most fascinated by the elephants. My trip to the zoo was one of the best experience I've ever had. I'm glad my brother forces me to get out of bed.

STOP

NYS Testing Program Answer Sheet

STUDENT'S NAME
LAST / FIRST / MI

SCHOOL:
TEACHER:
FEMALE ○   MALE ○

BIRTH DATE

MONTH	DAY	YEAR
Jan ○	⓪ ⓪	⓪ ⓪
Feb ○	① ①	① ①
Mar ○	② ②	② ②
Apr ○	③ ③	③ ③
May ○	④	④ ④
Jun ○	⑤	⑤ ⑤
Jul ○	⑥	⑥ ⑥
Aug ○	⑦	⑦ ⑦
Sep ○	⑧	⑧ ⑧
Oct ○	⑨	⑨ ⑨
Nov ○		
Dec ○		

GRADE ③ ④ ⑤ ⑥ ⑦ ⑧

Achieve New York State English Language Arts Grade 7

The New York State assessments in English Language Arts are published by CTB/McGraw-Hill. Such company has neither endorsed nor authorized this test-preparation book.

TEST
Book 1, Session 1

1 Ⓐ Ⓑ Ⓒ Ⓓ   6 Ⓕ Ⓖ Ⓗ Ⓙ   11 Ⓐ Ⓑ Ⓒ Ⓓ   16 Ⓕ Ⓖ Ⓗ Ⓙ   21 Ⓐ Ⓑ Ⓒ Ⓓ   26 Ⓕ Ⓖ Ⓗ Ⓙ
2 Ⓕ Ⓖ Ⓗ Ⓙ   7 Ⓐ Ⓑ Ⓒ Ⓓ   12 Ⓕ Ⓖ Ⓗ Ⓙ   17 Ⓐ Ⓑ Ⓒ Ⓓ   22 Ⓕ Ⓖ Ⓗ Ⓙ   27 Ⓐ Ⓑ Ⓒ Ⓓ
3 Ⓐ Ⓑ Ⓒ Ⓓ   8 Short response   13 Ⓐ Ⓑ Ⓒ Ⓓ   18 Ⓕ Ⓖ Ⓗ Ⓙ   23 Ⓐ Ⓑ Ⓒ Ⓓ   28 Short response
4 Ⓕ Ⓖ Ⓗ Ⓙ   9 Ⓐ Ⓑ Ⓒ Ⓓ   14 Ⓕ Ⓖ Ⓗ Ⓙ   19 Ⓐ Ⓑ Ⓒ Ⓓ   24 Ⓕ Ⓖ Ⓗ Ⓙ
5 Ⓐ Ⓑ Ⓒ Ⓓ   10 Ⓕ Ⓖ Ⓗ Ⓙ   15 Ⓐ Ⓑ Ⓒ Ⓓ   20 Ⓕ Ⓖ Ⓗ Ⓙ   25 Ⓐ Ⓑ Ⓒ Ⓓ

Book 2, Session 2

29 Ⓐ Ⓑ Ⓒ Ⓓ   34 Short response
30 Ⓕ Ⓖ Ⓗ Ⓙ
31 Ⓐ Ⓑ Ⓒ Ⓓ
32 Ⓕ Ⓖ Ⓗ Ⓙ
33 Short response

Answer short-response questions and make corrections to the editing task directly in the book.